Breaking the Dams

Breaking the Dams

The Story of Dambuster David Maltby and His Crew

*

Charles Foster

Pen & Sword
AVIATION

First published in Great Britain in 2008 by
Pen and Sword Aviation
An imprint of
Pen & Sword Books Ltd
47 Church Street
Barnsley
South Yorkshire
S70 2AS

ISBN 978 1 84415 686 3

A CIP catalogue record for this book is
available from the British Library

Designed and typeset in Scala and Today by Charles Foster
Printed and bound in England
By Biddles

Pen & Sword Books Ltd incorporates the Imprints of Pen & Sword Aviation,
Pen & Sword Family History, Pen & Sword Maritime, Pen & Sword Military,
Wharncliffe Local History, Pen & Sword Select, Pen & Sword Military Classics, Leo Cooper,
Remember When, Seaforth Publishing and Frontline Publishing

For a complete list of Pen & Sword titles please contact
PEN & SWORD BOOKS LIMITED
47 Church Street, Barnsley, South Yorkshire, S70 2AS, England
E-mail: enquiries@pen-and-sword.co.uk
Website: www.pen-and-sword.co.uk

Further information about this book on www.breakingthedams.com

Contents

*

In memory of

David Maltby DSO DFC
John Fort DFC
William Hatton
Victor Hill
Vivian Nicholson DFM
Harold Simmonds
Antony Stone

of the 1,394 people who died on the night of 16–17 May 1942

*of the 55,000 other members of RAF Bomber Command
who died between 1939 and 1945*

*and of my mother Jean Maltby,
her sister, Audrey,
and their parents, Ettrick and Aileen*

R I P

Note: The 1955 film and the Paul Brickhill book on which it is based, published in 1951, are both called *The Dam Busters*. However, the term Dambuster is more commonly seen these days, and I have chosen to use that in this text (except in specific references to the film or book title).

Prologue

*

Young, Happy and Beautiful

There's nothing glorious or noble about dying in war. It's a terrible tragedy which also affects, in many different ways, those who survive. But amongst those who took part in the Second World War, especially those who volunteered to fly in the RAF, there was a certain fatalism – an acceptance that death might come. It was well expressed by the Battle of Britain fighter-pilot Richard Hillary who survived severe burns after being shot down and wrote one of the best books about the war, *The Last Enemy*, while recuperating. Against medical advice he returned to flying and was killed in an accident. He wrote in a letter:

> ...we were not that stupid ... we could remember only too well that all this had been seen in the last war but, in spite of that and not because of it, we still thought this one worth fighting.[1]

This casualism – the ritual of the letter standing on the locker for the Committee of Adjustment Officer to post if you were killed – was hard for the families left behind to bear.

Mrs Elizabeth Nicholson, the mother of Flt Sgt Vivian Nicholson, soon after her son had been killed in the same tragedy as David Maltby, wrote movingly to David Maltby's father about a photograph taken in London on the day when the boys had both been decorated, three months earlier: 'It is indeed a terrible and deep wound for us when we look at them so young, happy and beautiful.' Words that are strikingly similar to those of the writer Iris Murdoch, in her novel *The Red and The Green*, describing the dead as being 'made young and perfect for ever.'[2] Murdoch's close friend Major Frank Thompson was killed in a Special Operations Executive (SOE) operation in Bulgaria in 1944 and,

1   Sebastian Faulks, *The Fatal Englishman*, Vintage, 1997, p.172
2   Iris Murdoch, *The Red and the Green*, Chatto, 1965

as her biographer notes, she was surely thinking of him as she wrote those words.[3]

Most of the seven young men who feature in this book were still teenagers, 'young, happy and beautiful', when they went to war. They weren't much older when they dropped the bomb which caused the final breach in the Möhne Dam on a moonlit night in May 1943, and then when they died just four months later. Each of them left a mother, a father, a brother or a sister; two of them had an infant child. This is their story.

3   Peter Conradi, *Iris Murdoch*, HarperCollins, 2001, p.195

Chapter 1

*

Introduction

I t's a piece of music that's as familiar as Rule Britannia or Over the Rainbow (and like them now downloadable as a ringtone for your mobile phone) but to us, growing up in the Home Counties in the late 1950s, it was indisputably – and slightly embarrassingly – our tune. If you sing that famous descending melody – 'daah-da-da-da-da' out loud in company, someone is bound to complete it... 'da, da-dee-da-da-da'. It instantly evokes an image: clean-shaven, bright-eyed young men putting one across the Jerries in a daring night-time raid. Or, perhaps, football fans in too-tight England jerseys urging their country on in another doomed penalty shoot-out. It is, of course, Eric Coates's music 'The Dam Busters March' first used in the 1955 film of the same name.

I can't remember when I first heard it – we had a scratchy 78 rpm record at home, played by the RAF Band, and it was often on the radio in the late 1950s. I know, however, that I didn't see the film itself until about 1961, when I was 11. During one school holiday my brother George and I were staying with my Aunt Audrey and Uncle Johnnie near Oxford. Together with our cousin, David, Audrey had driven us to some obscure cinema miles away (was it Abingdon? Aylesbury? Banbury?) because she had noticed that the film was showing. This time, instead of leaving us to sit through the screening on our own and collecting us afterwards, which was her usual practice when she took us to the pictures, Audrey came in with us. She paid sharp attention. 'Here it is,' she whispered to us as the scene began where Wg Cdr Guy Gibson, played by Richard Todd, and Gp Capt Charles Whitworth, played by Derek Farr, are shown leafing through an album full of photographs of aircrew, looking for pilots for the special mission. 'Oh yes, David Maltby,' says Whitworth and they pass on to the next page.

The film tells the rest of the story: a new RAF squadron is formed, 617 Squadron, led by Gibson. Their Lancaster bombers are specially adapted to carry a secret new weapon, the so-called 'bouncing bomb', designed to attack several large dams in the Ruhr valley, the heart of Germany's industrial region. But when they attack the first dam things don't go exactly to plan. Four aircraft attack, one crashes in flames, but the dam is still in place. David Maltby is piloting the next plane. 'Hello J-Johnny are you ready?' asks Gibson. 'OK Leader,' says the actor George Baker, playing David. Then there is silence as his aircraft approaches, two others flying ahead of him to draw the flak. The bomb is dropped, bounces four, five, six times – then a pause, followed by an explosion at the base of the dam. Still the soundtrack remains silent, but, just as the next aircraft is lining up, someone shouts out, 'It's gone, look, my God!' A rush of water through the dam – and a blast of music.

In the cinema that day a prickle of recognition ran down the back of my neck, a feeling that I have had countless times since. Even at 11, I knew well what connected my family to this story because I had read, and reread, Paul Brickhill's book which shares the name of the film. The pilot who dropped the bomb which broke the dam, David Maltby, was my uncle – the only brother of my Aunt Audrey and my mother, Jean.

At the age of 23 David had been a bomber pilot for almost two years. He had completed one tour of operations and been awarded a DFC before he took part in the raid. He had been selected to fly in this new squadron set up specifically to destroy a target the Germans believed to be nearly impregnable. After six weeks of training he had flown in the first wave of bombers that had left a bumpy, grass runway in Lincolnshire on a bright May evening, piloting a plane with the code letters AJ-J, J for Johnny. For his role in the operation, he was decorated with a DSO.

Four months after the Dams Raid he was dead, leaving a wife, Nina, and a ten-week-old baby son, John. His aircraft went down in the North Sea, his body was brought ashore in Suffolk by an Air Sea Rescue launch and he was buried in Kent, in the church in which he had been married 16 months before.

We had a number of mementoes of David around the house. A reproduction of a drawing by Cuthbert Orde, published as part of a double page spread in *The Tatler*, a photograph of him meeting the King (my mother always pointing out the bulge in his tunic pocket where he had stuffed his pipe and tobacco). I would look at these and notice how much David resembled my mother – the same roundness in the cheeks, the nose and chin, the height.

His height is the first thing that everyone remembers as their first impression. In his book *Enemy Coast Ahead*, Guy Gibson, who was himself originally turned down for the RAF as too short, calls him 'tall and thoughtful',[4] and in the 617 Squadron photos you can see him towering over most of the others. The Maltbys are a tall family – Audrey and Jean were both 5 ft 10 in, and Ettrick, their father and my grandfather, was well over 6 ft.

George Baker, who played David in the film, is also a tall man, and confirmed to me in 2006 that the casting director Robert Leonard and film director Michael Anderson had tried to find lookalike actors to play the various parts.

> On the desk in front of them they had a photo of [David] and one of me and I must admit that there was a considerable similarity. Then when I met Group Captain Whitworth he fell into the habit of calling me Dave, which was really quite disconcerting.

This is the same Whitworth whose screen character was supposed to have picked David out of an album. During the war Whitworth had been the station commander at RAF Scampton, and when the film was being made he was asked to become the technical adviser. In a 2005 radio interview,[5] George Baker told a story about David being so wound up after a raid that he used to shoot china plates with his service revolver to relieve the tension. He heard this story from Whitworth:

> [Whitworth] would often refer to an incident thinking that I had been there. This is how the story of the plate shooting came to be told, quite obviously the men of the squadron became extremely tense before and after an operational flight but other indications from the Group Captain told me that he was a very funny man and a delightful companion. I feel very honoured to have had the chance to portray him in the film.[6]

Because George Baker had played our uncle, our family 'adopted' him – when we were growing up we would look out for him in films or on TV. He turned up in various Wednesday Plays, episodes of *Z Cars* and

4 Guy Gibson, *Enemy Coast Ahead*, Michael Joseph 1946, p.242
5 BBC Radio 4, Today, 13 December 2005
6 George Baker, Email to author, 17 May 2006

Up Pompeii, before appearing in a couple of James Bond films and *I Claudius*. Now, of course, he's best known as Chief Inspector Wexford in the *Ruth Rendell Mysteries* TV series.

The scene in the film where Gibson and Whitworth select the pilots for the raid is actually complete fiction. It derives from Gibson's own account in his book *Enemy Coast Ahead,* except that in the book he says that he gave the names of the pilots he wanted to a 'fellow with a red moustache' called Cartwright. Whitworth was not involved at all.[7] In reality, Gibson asked for some pilots by name, but they were mainly those he had flown with previously. Other Lancaster squadrons – including the squadron with which David was flying in March 1943 – were asked to recommend experienced pilots and David obviously fitted the bill. David had never served with Gibson up to this point. It is possible that their paths had crossed in some officers' mess or other, but I have never found any evidence of this.

Other fictional scenes were also added to the film for dramatic effect: the most famous being when Gibson and one of his crew are supposed to get the idea for using spotlights to gauge the aircraft's height over water from a visit to the theatre. In reality the idea to use spotlights came from an Air Ministry scientist.

But no matter. *The Dam Busters* was released on the twelfth anniversary of the raid itself, in May 1955, and was an immediate box-office success. The interest lies not only in the tale but also its timing and, 'the manner of its telling, which reinforced the nostalgic optimism of Britain in the 1950s before Suez: 'Churchill back in Downing Street, Everest conquered, a new sovereign', writes Richard Morris.[8] But for some, the depiction of their loved one on screen was too much. My grandparents turned down their invitation to the premiere, choosing to see the film quietly and anonymously some time later when it came on general release.

The actual raid and the film have become so conflated in people's minds that it is perhaps no surprise that truth and fiction are sometimes confused. A mini-industry in 'collectables' has sprung up around the Dambusters and it does its best to further the confusion by offering for sale as items of equal importance 'Dambuster tribute' prints, first-day-cover envelopes and other artefacts signed either by one of the few men still alive who flew on the raid – or by Richard Todd, Guy Gibson's celluloid equivalent. Thus for £40 you can get a print signed by Todd (a

7   Gibson, *Enemy Coast Ahead*, p.239
8   Richard Morris, *Guy Gibson*, Penguin 1995, p.315

fine fellow who had a distinguished war career, but still an *actor,* playing a real life RAF pilot) or by George Johnson, the real-life bombaimer who dropped a bomb on the Sorpe Dam and won a DFM for his efforts. (£40 is at the bottom end of the celebrity scale. You need to pay almost twice as much for a Manchester United print signed by Wayne Rooney.)

Even the most peripheral connections to the Dambusters legend are exploited. A pub near 617 Squadron's wartime base at RAF Scampton, in the Lincolnshire village of the same name, which had no pub at all in the Second World War, was until recently a 'living tribute to the legendary "Dambusters" of the Royal Air Force' where you could enjoy the 'convivial atmosphere that exists within its limestone walls – walls that are adorned with a marvellous and poignant collection of Royal Air Force WW2 memorabilia.' This pub has now closed, the reason perhaps being what one bulletin board correspondent noted as its rather unwelcoming atmosphere. However, the owners obviously thought they were convivial enough hosts. They were very proud of the fact that you could dig out your battledress or utility skirt and recreate the wartime mood as a member of a local '1940s Re-enactment Group' which met there to 'add flavour' to the locals' Sunday lunchtime pints. It was almost enough to make you choke on your powdered egg.

The arrival of the internet has further fuelled Dambuster mania. There are dozens of websites with material about 617 Squadron and its exploits, many repeating the same inaccurate information. Some websites can tell me the registration number of the Lancaster aircraft that David flew to the Dams, but can't get other things right – the correct spelling of his father's name being an obvious example.

Working on this book, however, has made me realise that there is a lot I simply don't know. I remember many of the stories that my mother told us about the war, but she has been dead for 20 years. Her tendency to over-embroider any narrative got worse towards the end of her life, and now I wonder whether she made some of it up completely. She once told my brother Andrew that she had been taken by the police to identify David's body. But I never heard this from her myself, as either a child or an adult.

So I began the work by trying to put together a better picture of the rest of the crew of AJ-J. Their names were familiar to me from the aircrew lists in my mother's copy of Guy Gibson's *Enemy Coast Ahead,* but it takes a bit more research to find out more than just their ranks and surnames. The crew that flew with David on the Dams Raid – or to give it its official name, Operation Chastise – were:

Flight Engineer:	Sgt William Hatton
Navigator:	Sgt Vivian Nicholson
Wireless Operator:	Sgt Antony Stone
Bomb Aimer:	Plt Off John Fort
Front Gunner:	Sgt Victor Hill
Rear Gunner:	Sgt Harold Simmonds.

There is one invaluable guide to anyone trying to find out more about Operation Chastise. John Sweetman's 1982 book, revised in 2002 as *The Dambusters Raid,* is the most authoritative account of all, and, as I am later to discover, much more reliable than those accounts which purport to be 'definitive'. As regards the crews, he quickly debunks the myth that they were all veterans and hand-picked by Gibson:

> ... the majority were not decorated (including six of the pilots); and far from having finished two operational tours some had not done one. Many who would fly to the German dams in May 1943 had completed fewer than ten operations against enemy targets.[9]

In fact, David Maltby's crew was probably the most inexperienced of the lot. Three of them, Nicholson, Stone and Simmonds, had never flown on an operation at all. John Fort and William Hatton had only flown a handful. David, by contrast, had done a full operational tour of 28 flights in 106 and 97 Squadrons between June 1941 and June 1942. After a few months on the usual between-tours break, in his case commanding a target and gunnery flight, training bomb aimers and gunners, he had gone back for a second tour. It was on his return to 97 Squadron in March 1943 that he met the five who were to be his crew: all waiting to start work. They crewed-up together but were then transferred the few miles from Coningsby to Scampton, to the new 617 Squadron to begin the special training. Another front gunner originally came with them, but he was replaced by Victor Hill only 10 days before the actual raid. He brought some real operational experience to the crew, having flown on more than 20 sorties in 9 Squadron.

---

9   John Sweetman, *The Dambusters Raid*, Cassell, 2002, p.98

During the training for the Dams Raid the crew of AJ-J obviously came in for some ribbing from the rest for being so inexperienced. The Squadron's Adjutant, Harry Humphries, says that David himself used to call them 'sprogs' and 'rookies'.[10] However, they acquitted themselves admirably when put to the test. So well, in fact, that navigator Vivian Nicholson and bomb aimer John Fort were decorated on their first and second missions respectively.

This same crew flew together on just three more sorties over the next four months until on 15 September 1943, turning back when recalled from a low-level operation to bomb the Dortmund Ems canal, some sort of accident occurred and the aircraft plunged into the North Sea. Only David's body was ever found – the rest must still be trapped in the broken fuselage hundreds of feet below the surface.

It seems to have been a happy crew, but they had no illusions about how difficult their jobs were and the risks involved. In the letter left for his family, which they received after the fatal crash, wireless operator Sgt Antony Stone wrote: 'I will have ended happily, so have no fears of how I ended as I have the finest crowd of fellows with me, and if the skipper goes I will be glad to go with him. He has so much to lose, far more responsibilities than I.'[11]

What have the obsessions of website researchers and harmless 're-enactment' charades to do with the real Second World War – a war in which hundreds of thousands of British people, and perhaps forty-five million people worldwide, lost their lives? At each of these deaths, a family was bereaved. A son or a daughter, a brother or sister, an aunt or an uncle – each loss affected someone else. For many of the generation who survived, the war became something they were not able to talk about: it was too painful. The writer Ivy Compton Burnett could not read the war trilogy in Anthony Powell's *Dance to the Music of Time* novels, 'finding any reference to war unbearable after the death in action of a much beloved brother'.[12] Her feelings were shared by many others.

In my family, the loss that was felt all through their lives by my mother, her sister and her parents, Ettrick and Aileen, not to mention David's wife and baby son, was tempered by the undoubted pride they felt in him. He had been decorated twice, had taken part in one of the

10   Harry Humphries, *Living with Heroes*, Erskine Press, 2003, p.34
11   Stone family correspondence
12   Anthony Powell, *To Keep the Ball Rolling*, Penguin, 1983, p.341

most spectacular events of the war and, later, immortalised in a film complete with stirring music. No wonder that, as children, we were brought up with the legend, shown the pictures and the medals, encouraged to read the book – and to write in to *Children's Favourites* on the Light Programme requesting the record.

David wasn't the only person in my mother's family to be killed in the war. Of the nearly 580,000 British and Commonwealth people who died, three more were her first cousins – Ralph Maltby, Louis Maltby and Charles Bartlet. Ralph Maltby, who was also Ettrick's god-son, was a Captain in the Royal Artillery and died at Arnhem in September 1944. Louis Maltby had been born and brought up in South Africa. A Lieutenant in the Kimberley Regiment, he was wounded while fighting in Italy, captured by the Germans, and died as a PoW in November 1944.

On the other side of her family, a fearful symmetry occurred. My grandmother, Aileen, had an older sister, Mildred Bartlet, and she also had one son and two daughters. Charles Bartlet and David Maltby were born a few months apart in 1920 and spent many holidays together as boys. As neither had a brother they were very close. David died in September 1943 and Charles, a Lieutenant in the Irish Guards, died at Anzio just five months later. I remember Great Aunt Mildred only as my grandmother's rather severe and a bit scary older sister. No wonder she seemed forbidding. As children we often treat our elders with indifference, but now I shudder when I think of what this pair of sis-ters, who had also lost a brother in the trenches in the First World War, must have gone through.

Growing up in the 1950s and early 1960s meant that it was impossi-ble to escape the Second World War, even though I was born five years after it finished. Not only were there the experiences of our parents and other relatives (my father, already in the navy as an officer cadet before the war started, finally saw active service in the Indian Ocean in 1943), there was also the never-ending stream of other cultural material. I was a great reader as a child, and used to devour comics like the *Wizard* and the *Victor*, which contained lots of real-life war stories, as well as the small format Battle Picture Library and War Picture Library comic magazines. Then there were the proper books – *The Great Escape, Reach for the Sky,* and *One of Our Submarines* (a particular favourite of mine, written by Edward Young, who designed the very first Penguin

Books). There were also the films – *Reach for the Sky* (again), *Sink the Bismarck* and *The Guns of Navarone*. Even our playthings – Eighth Army plastic soldiers, Airfix models, old Army tin helmets rescued from jumble sales- recreated the war.

But as we grew older, memories of the war began to change, almost imperceptibly at first. In 1963, aged 13, I went away to St Edward's School in Oxford, where Ettrick, my grandfather, had been in the 1890s. This was the same school at which Guy Gibson, later to be David's commanding officer in 617 Squadron, had been a pupil in the 1930s. By the time I arrived Gibson was commemorated in some style – as the school's only VC he had his own memorial window in the chapel. The school had other famous war heroes, notably Douglas Bader, the subject of *Reach for the Sky*. He, of course, survived the war, and was frequently seen making his jerky way around the Quad at the Gaudy speech day.

These were the well-known ones, but, as in most English public schools, you didn't have to be famous to be commemorated – just dead. The names of hundreds of young men were carved in stone on the rolls of honour on the chapel walls and I spent many a boring sermon idly reading the inscriptions at the end of my pew. Every November, on Remembrance Sunday, our regular service was moved outside, and we would stand in the cold while wreaths were laid on the war memorial. As the chapel clock struck 11 I would try and picture David, the uncle I never knew, during the two minute silence that followed.

By the time I went away to school, my grandparents were getting on. They celebrated their golden wedding a year later in 1964, and had the usual photographs taken for the local papers in Northamptonshire. (My father, slightly exasperated by them at times, read the press cuttings and complained, to me at least but probably not to my mother, that they had managed to 'bring up the Dambusters again'.) Then, at the beginning of 1967, they both died, quite quickly and within a few months of each other. Ettrick, who never seemed in the best of health but was then 82 years old, took to his bed after Christmas and died in late January. Then Aileen was diagnosed with lung cancer, and died in April. The ever present Gold Leaf cigarettes, balanced Andy Capp-like in one corner of her mouth for so long that she had developed a yellow nicotine stain on the side of her hair, had caught up with her. She had never smoked before David died.

As their generation passed, gentle mocking of the war began to be more acceptable. I doubt very much that my grandparents ever saw *Beyond the Fringe,* but extracts from it were shown on TV sometime in the 1960s, and I remember being discomfited at the moment when Peter Cook tells Jonathan Miller:

> I want you to lay down your life, Perkins. We need a futile gesture at this stage. It will raise the whole tone of the war. Get up in a crate, Perkins, pop over to Bremen, take a shufti, don't come back. Goodbye Perkins. I wish I was going too.[13]

The late 1960s and early 1970s saw the enormous success of TV programmes like *Dad's Army,* which glossed over the war's horrors and mocked pomposity and bureaucracy in a cosy, unthreatening way. Other programmes found it easy to adopt a sharper tone. The catch phrase 'Don't mention the war' is funny when uttered by barking mad Torquay hoteliers, but it must still have evoked difficult memories for people who loved and lost.

But then there came a further slight shift in the public's attitude. It began with the realisation that a generation was dying and that, perhaps, not enough was being done. From 1989, the anniversaries started in earnest. The commemoration of the occasion of 50 years since the start of the war, started a cycle of golden anniversaries: the Battle of Britain, Pearl Harbor, El Alamein, D-Day, VE Day, Hiroshima, VJ Day. The cycle went round again with the 60th anniversaries but by 2005 it became clear that on each of these occasions, the people who had direct experience – the ranks of bemedalled British Legion members standing still as the sound of Nimrod swelled in the chill November air – were diminishing. So up stepped the kids. In came the school projects, the People's History archives, the museum living exhibits. Asking your granddad about the war became a national pastime. So much so that people now complain that for the British schoolchild modern history seems to consist of the Second World War and little else.

✳ ✳ ✳

Ettrick Maltby and Aileen Hatfeild were married on 28 July 1914, shortly before Ettrick's thirtieth birthday. Ettrick was the fourth of five child-

---

13 Roger Wilmut ed, *The Complete Beyond the Fringe,* Methuen, 1987, p.74

ren, and his father and grandfather were both clergymen. He was born in Aspley, Bedfordshire, where his father was the vicar. Family legend says that he derived his unusual Christian name from the river in Scotland where his father was on holiday fishing when he got the word his son was born. (A true sportsman as well as a man of the cloth, he is reputed to have finished landing the salmon he had hooked before making his way to his wife's bedside.) After being sent to St Edward's, a school founded in 1863 to cater for the sons of the impoverished clergy, Ettrick had taken another step on this traditional educational path and went up to Keble College, Oxford, where he was good at sport, winning a Blue for hockey and a half-Blue for golf. After leaving Oxford he started teaching at a preparatory school in Kent.

Ettrick may have come from a line of poor vicars, but Aileen's family were quite prosperous, from a well-connected family in Margate, the Hatfeilds (spelt in this unusual way). They were active in local politics, Conservatives naturally, and both her parents served on Margate Council. Aileen's mother, Maud Back, aged 25, had married her cousin Charles Hatfeild, who was already 50, in September 1885. They had seven children in quick succession, of whom Aileen was the fifth, and the second daughter. Charles Hatfeild died in 1910, at the age of 74.

Aileen had only just turned 19 when she and Ettrick were married on 28 July 1914. Perhaps Maud didn't find this too much of a problem, given that there had been an even larger age gap between her and her husband. Sport may have been what brought Ettrick and Aileen together for, like Ettrick, Aileen was good at games. Under his tutelage she also took up hockey, becoming a goalkeeper like him, and was eventually capped for England several times in the 1920s.

For some reason, presumably to do with his health, Ettrick didn't go into the forces during the First World War. As he had turned 30 on 12 August 1914, he was certainly too old to be conscripted. After their marriage, he and Aileen moved first to Willingdon, near Eastbourne. He had a job teaching in a school named Hydneye House after the road in which it was situated, The Hydneye. Their first daughter, Audrey, was born there on 26 June 1917.

In July 1918, the school moved to a large redbrick Victorian house in a village called Baldslow, near Hastings, in an area known locally as The Ridge. The house was renamed Hydneye House and Ettrick became joint headmaster of the school. It was there that their other two children were born: David, on 10 May 1920, and Jean, my mother, on 30 December 1924.

They were to stay at Hydneye House for 37 years with a short interruption during the war when it was requisitioned by the army. We often spent family holidays there in the first five years of my life and I remember it well as an impressive country house style residence – you swept up a drive past a gate lodge to an open space in front of the house, itself fronted by a big lawn overlooked by two giant cedar trees. Inside, large rooms opened up off a wood-panelled hall, with a big staircase lifting you gracefully to the first floor.

Doubtless it was a great place to grow up as a child. Certainly my mother always talked of it nostalgically and was very upset when it was demolished in the 1970s to make way for a comprehensive school. In the 1980s more development took place in the area and a new district hospital, the Conquest Hospital, was opened almost opposite where the school once stood. It was in this hospital that my mother died, in July 1987, and she was cremated a short distance further along The Ridge, at Hastings Crematorium. So, she was born, died and her ashes were scattered in three separate places, just a few hundred yards apart.

It turns out that my grandfather kept a diary all his life, and it is now in the possession of my cousin Anthea. She told me on the phone that the entries are very short but that it seemed to run from the 1920s through to the 1960s. A few weeks later, sitting in her kitchen in Edinburgh, I was able to examine it. It is a five year diary, with thick, smooth paper bound in a pale brown rough artificial moleskin. It was given to him by someone called Bill Mallory, according to the bookplate pasted carefully on the flyleaf. Ever economical, Ettrick obviously decided to make use of it for as many years as he could, and recorded events on its pages over four decades, which makes it rather confusing to follow. Some pages have got many entries, each for separate years from the 1920s to the 1960s, others very few. And the entries vary in their content – recording family movements and events, appointments of staff at the school, current affairs ('Chamberlain flies to Munich'), the weather, race meetings, cricket scores and gardening records. Mainly in pencil, it's all written in his neat, rather feminine hand which I remember from my childhood.

I realised that the only way of making sense of the diary would be to type it up myself in chronological order but, in the meantime, Anthea and I occupied ourselves by looking up days on which we thought he would have recorded something of interest. Her birthday – 27 March – has a number of entries, which include:

> 1930: A[ileen] & I to Belper.
> 1941: Tropical rain at Witherdon. D[avid] motored down from Oxford. Inspected craters.
> 1943: Became Granpop! Anthea born 1.30pm at Southborne, T.Wells
> 1945: A & I left Witherdon for good + trailer & hens! And home about 7pm & found Jean at Tanner's lodge where we lived & pigged for about 10 days.

I was most interested, of course, in the war years, in which Witherdon features a lot. Hydneye had been evacuated to this large house near Okehampton in Devon in 1940. By 1945, they were obviously relieved to be on the way home, even though the war was not yet over.

The arrival of a fifth grandchild, me, on 4 January 1950 is celebrated more prosaically:

> 4 January 1950: A to Worthing. Charles born Malta.

David, of course, features many times. A little nervously, I turned to the dates that I know will be important. How much detail did he record?

> 16 May 1943: (16th & 17th) Great 'Dam' raid in which David took part & won the D.S.O. (29)

And then, curiously, underneath but with a pencil arrow placing it above the first line, he wrote:

> 1942: D over Copenhagen (Gardening 24)

This would imply he wrote the 1942 entry *after* that for 1943. As I flicked through the pages, I saw other German cities mentioned, each accompanied by a circled or underlined number:

> 15 Jan 1942: D over Hamburg. (17) 1190 incendiaries! in a Manchester

(1st pilot)
27 April 1942: D over Trondheim (19) Tirpitz
3 May 1942: D shot up over Dunkirk & had to do a horrible crash landing at Coningsby (Stuttgart 21)

The numbers must refer to the running total of operations completed,
and the occasional incorrect sequence shows that he obviously did not
write every entry exactly on the day it occurred. However it was still
going to be a very useful, almost contemporary, record of key events.

I began to wonder how he got this information. Was David ringing
or writing to his parents every time he completed an operation? That
seemed unlikely. Or did Ettrick write them all up at one time, later, perhaps after he died?

I turned to September, and the sequence of dates which must have
been terrible for him to record:

15 September 1943: David, approx: 1 A.M. – we had the news at 3.30p.m.

This was written in a dark pencil. Then underneath, in his customary
lighter pencil, obviously written later:

It was his 33rd op. trip – most of his big ones had been done in Lanc.
906, but this was 981.
813 hrs–20mins.

He can't have known these details on the day of the crash, but he was
right. I knew when I read these words that on the raid on which he
died, which was aborted mid-operation, David wasn't flying the Lancaster which had taken him safely to the Dams and back, but another
newer aircraft, No. JA981. His Dams Raid aircraft, Lancaster No.
EE906, call sign AJ-J, must have been a lucky plane. It survived the war
and was eventually scrapped in 1947. Lancaster JA981 had only flown
for 41 hours before it crashed. As I read I puzzled over how and when
Ettrick had managed to get hold of the serial numbers of his aircraft, let
alone the total number of hours David had flown in his RAF career.

On 17 September 1943, they left Devon for the long drive to Kent for
the funeral. Ettrick wrote:

Left Witherdon to go to Hemel. Audrey & Anthea arrd. there from
B'head.

This was a Friday. Aileen's youngest sister Violet lived in Hemel
Hempstead, where her husband Ted was the village doctor. I know
from the newspaper cuttings that they were all at the funeral, which
took place the following day:

18 September 1943: David's funeral at Wickhambreaux. A went to
Hengrove afterwards – we retd to Hemel with Audrey & Johnnie.

Why did Aileen go to her brother's house at Hengrove in Kent, while
the others – Audrey, Johnnie and presumably my mother who doesn't
get a mention but who I know was at the funeral – went back to Hemel
Hempstead? Whatever the reason, two days later they returned to
Devon, where the school term was about to start:

20 September 1943: Milner-Everitt & Miss Hook joined staff. Returned
to Witherdon to find 84 letters waiting for us.

News travelled fast, even in wartime. David's crash had occurred in the
early hours of Wednesday morning, and he was buried on the Saturday.
Many people had probably seen the notice in *The Times*, but that had
only appeared on the morning of the funeral.

For most of the rest of September 1943 very little is recorded.
Aileen's sister Mildred Bartlet and her daughter Frances, who had a
small child, couldn't go to the funeral but visited them at Witherdon
shortly afterwards. Sixty-three years later Frances told me how she
remembers Aileen and Ettrick sitting, still in shock, in separate parts of
the garden. Their daughter Audrey said to her: 'The problem with
Mummy and Daddy is that they can't console each other.'

I left Edinburgh with a complete photocopy of all the pages, and
started the long task of typing them up in order.

✳   ✳   ✳

Another series of phone calls put me in touch with some more valuable
sources of information. I spoke first to Terry Rogers, the archivist at

Marlborough College and was taken aback when he told me that 241 boys from the school were killed in the Second World War, at a time when there were about 500 boys in the school. (That huge number is itself dwarfed by the 742 who died in the First World War.) Also he mentioned that there were two Marlburians on the Dams Raid, the other being Flt Lt John Hopgood, the pilot of AJ-M, the second aircraft to attempt a strike on the dam, and shot down with the loss of all but two of the crew. Terry told me that he got a lot of help from another archivist called Alex Bateman, who apparently is an expert on the men who took part in the operation.

When I rang Alex Bateman it turned out that not only did he have a file full of stuff about David Maltby but he also had an enormous archive of material which he has been collecting for nigh on twenty years, and he was generous with his time and help. In the bundle of stuff he sent me later that week were a number of gems, including a photo of the whole crew, taken at RAF Blida in Algeria in the summer of 1943. He had been given this by Mrs Grace Blackburn, the sister of Sgt Harold Simmonds, the rear gunner. I pored over the picture: David I recognised straightaway, the tallest of course, fourth from the left in a pair of service khaki shorts and long socks. The rest I don't know, but a note confirms the line up. Front gunner Vic Hill is on the left, in long service trousers and flying boots. Antony Stone, the wireless operator, is next, thin and bare-chested. Bomb aimer John Fort, the oldest of the group, is on the left of David. To his right is flight engineer William Hatton, in a rather dashing cravat. Harold Simmonds is on the end, a cowlick of dark hair falling over his face, and wearing a huge pair of trousers that start halfway down his chest. Crouching in front is the young Vivian Nicholson, who won the DFM in his first raid, navigating AJ-J safely to the Möhne Dam and back.

I thought of what I then knew of them all, aided by some books and their entries at the Commonwealth War Graves Commission website. Hill: a gardener's son from Gloucestershire. Stone: whose father was a barber in Winchester; some of his old customers still remember him – he kept a portrait of his son in his shop until he retired. Stone's mother had turned up in Harry Humphries' office the day after Stone was killed, repeating over and over, 'Did he suffer? Did he suffer?'[14] Fort: from Lancashire and the oldest at 31, who had been in the RAF since 1932. Hatton: a Yorkshireman from Wakefield. Simmonds: a Sussex

---

14 Humphries, *Living with Heroes*, p. 61

The crew who flew Lancaster AJ-J on the Dams Raid, pictured in Blida, Algeria, some time between 15 and 24 July 1943. Standing, left to right: Sgt Victor Hill (front gunner), Sgt Antony Stone (wireless operator), Plt Off John Fort DFC (bomb aimer), Sqn Ldr David Maltby DSO DFC (pilot), Sgt William Hatton (flight engineer), Sgt Harold Simmonds (rear gunner). Crouching: Sgt Vivian Nicholson DFM (navigator). PHOTO: GRACE BLACKBURN

boy like David, who had a girlfriend called Phyllis. Nicholson: who came from County Durham, and had been shipped across the Atlantic to Canada to do his navigator's training.

I had also been able to reach Robert Owen, the official historian of 617 Squadron. He told me more about the Dambusters who are still alive and contacts them on my behalf. Over the next few weeks I received letters or emails from four of them. It's a humbling experience receiving these notes – these are all men in their mid or late 80s, and they are uniformly courteous, even though they are repeating stories that they must have told hundreds of times before. They all remembered David and were able to pass on some useful information.

Two of them live in Canada: Fred Sutherland and Grant MacDonald, both gunners, who flew in Les Knight's and Ken Brown's aircraft respectively. Fred Sutherland sent me a long email with some detail about the night David's plane went down. He mentioned that he himself was shot down over Holland the very next day, 16 September 1943, but baled out and eventually got home with the help of the Dutch resistance. Les Knight, his pilot, died that day, heroically struggling to maintain height long enough so that the rest of the crew could bale out. It was a terrible day for 617 Squadron: in four of the other eight crews all the members were killed outright. Fred Sutherland also mentioned that he knew Vic Hill quite well, and had been in touch with a friend of Hill's daughter a few years back. He dug out an old address for the friend, and eventually I obtained the phone number for Valerie Ashton, née Hill.

Valerie is therefore the first relative of a member of David's crew that I actually spoke to. She was two when her father died and has a vague memory of being taken to the railway station by her mother to say goodbye to him. Her mother remarried after the war and so she was brought up by a new stepfather. She now regrets not finding out more about her real father before her mother died. But she has turned up some material including letters and photographs.

The only surviving pilot from the Dams Raid is Les Munro, who went back to New Zealand after the war. His long email, answering all my questions, is full of nuggets of information. Like David, he had previously been in 97 Squadron, but when he joined it in the autumn of 1942, David was serving in the Target and Gunnery flight on his between-tours break. Ten days after David came back to start a second tour they were both transferred to 617 Squadron.

✳   ✳   ✳

Immediately the war started David left his job in mining, travelled down from Yorkshire and tried to sign up for the RAF. Ettrick recorded in his diary on 8 September 1939 that David 'went to Brighton to enlist but wasn't wanted!'. He eventually managed to join the RAFVR (the RAF Volunteer Reserve) in March 1940, but wasn't actually called up until 20 June. The sheer logistics of getting more than a quarter of a million new recruits into the service must have almost overwhelmed it, and David obviously just had to wait his turn.

It's worth recalling just what a state the country was in at the time that he finally got his call-up papers. Churchill had been Prime Minister for little more than a month. He had almost broken down in the car on the way back to Admiralty House after being appointed by the King at Buckingham Palace. When his bodyguard, Inspector Thompson, congratulated him saying that he knew he had an enormous task, he replied, with tears in his eyes, 'God alone knows how great it is. I hope it is not too late. I am very much afraid it is. We can only do our best.' As John Lukacs has noted, Hitler's advance not only seemed irresistible: in many places and many ways it was.[15]

Churchill made two of his greatest speeches in that month. On Tuesday 4 June he told a silent House of Commons about the fall of France, Belgium and the retreat from Dunkirk. He spoke of how it might be necessary to fight to defend 'our island home', ending with his famous peroration: 'we shall fight on the beaches, we shall fight on the landing grounds, we shall fight in the fields and in the streets, we shall fight in the hills; we shall never surrender...'. Oratory on a grand scale, designed to rouse the nation. He had to wind up his gift for inspirational language again, just a fortnight later when his words were broadcast once more. This time he warned the listening world that the Battle of Britain was about to begin: 'Let us therefore brace ourselves to our duties, and so bear ourselves that, if the British Empire and Commonwealth last for a thousand years, men will still say, "This was their finest hour."'

It's curious how oratory has the power to influence a national mood. Just a few days after I had looked up these words and typed them out, a CD of great speeches popped out of my copy of *The Guardian* one Saturday. Included in it was the earlier, post-Dunkirk speech. Even now you can hear the determination in Churchill's voice, the whole massive backing of power and resolve behind his words like a fortress: they are never words for words' sake. As Simon Schama wrote in an accompanying essay, referring to a contemporary article by Vita Sackville-West: 'They were words for everyone's sake. They were the lifeboat and the blood transfusion. They turned the tide.'[16]

The day after Churchill's deep growl resonated from a million wireless sets, David set off from Okehampton railway station for a reception centre at RAF Uxbridge. New aircrew were badly needed: even though the Battle of Britain had not yet started, bomber pilots in inadequate aircraft were already falling like flies. (Max Hastings tells the

15   John Lukacs, *Five Days in London*, Yale 2001, p.6
16   Simon Schama, *Great Speeches of the 20th Century No.1*, *The Guardian* pamphlet, 2007

story of one called 'Ten Minute' Jenkins who was shot down on his first operation before he had even unpacked his kitbag.[17])

By September 1940 Churchill had already identified the expansion of Bomber Command as the key to victory. He wrote in a memorandum to Lord Beaverbrook:

> The Navy can lose us the war, but only the Air Force can win it. Therefore our supreme effort must be to gain overwhelming mastery in the air. The Fighters are our salvation, but the Bombers alone provide the means of victory.[18]

When Churchill wrote those words it was by no means clear that Britain, then standing alone although bolstered by its forces from the Commonwealth, would emerge victorious. In the end, of course, it did – but at the price of the lives of more than 55,000 Bomber Command aircrew. These would include the seven young men in Grace Blackburn's picture, a casual snap taken in the unaccustomed heat and dust of North Africa. Two months after the picture was taken, and four months after taking part in the most famous single bombing operation of the war, they were all dead.

17 Max Hastings, *Bomber Command*, Michael Joseph, 1979, p.69
18 John Terraine, *The Right of the Line*, Hodder & Stoughton, 1985, p.260

Chapter 2

In Memoriam

I f there was an organisation that searched the countryside for the archetypal English village for films then Wickhambreaux in Kent would score highly. It has buildings in a mixture of redbrick, flint and white weatherboard, a village green overlooked by a grand house, a Church, a pub and an olde worlde mill. The village is in one of Kent's most beautiful valleys, that of the River Stour, and lies five or so miles east of Canterbury.

On one day in September every year a small group of elderly men gather in the village. Smartly dressed in blazers and sporting ties with a propeller motif, they order their lunch from the menu at The Rose pub and then, accompanied by their ladies, cross the roughly cut green to the iron wicket-gate in front of St Andrew's Church. One at a time, they pull back the gate's stiff hinges and walk the few yards to a low grave next to the War Memorial. A few other people are present: mostly elderly, others in various stages of middle age who are perhaps slightly too young to remember the war, but would have heard their parents tell of it. One of the gathering speaks, reading from a script typed in capitals on a manual typewriter. He invites another to lay a wreath, who steps forward and, stooping slightly awkwardly, places a red, white and blue roundel on the grave. They all bow their heads for a few moments silence.

The place where this little ceremony is enacted each year was actually once the location for a real film. During the summer and autumn of 1943 Michael Powell and Emeric Pressburger shot several scenes for their film *A Canterbury Tale* in the village of Wickhambreaux and, as the camera crews and actors took their positions for the scenes filmed in the churchyard, they must surely have noticed the fresh earth and fading flowers that marked the cemetery's newest incumbent. For it

Wickhambreaux as it must have looked in the 1930s from a contemporary postcard.   PHOTO: PAUL TRITTON

was here, a week before, that David Maltby had been laid to rest. St Andrew's was the parish church of his parents-in-law, George and Hilda Goodson, who had a farm called Frognall, just outside the village. It was the same church where he had married his wife, Nina, 16 months earlier. It's a small but attractive church built in the 14th century and extensively restored in Victorian times. The huge Art Nouveau stained-glass east window dates from that restoration. It is the work of an American glass manufacturer and was installed in the church in memory of a wealthy American woman, Harriet Duer Gallatin, who is also buried in the graveyard.

Right next to the church is the village's grandest house, Wickhambreaux Court. In the 1940s this was the home of Frank and Elizabeth Montgomery. The house was used in the film *A Canterbury Tale* as the home of the mysterious local magistrate, Thomas Colpepper, with the Montgomerys themselves appearing as extras in some scenes. In the film when the character called Alison (played by Sheila

Sim, who later married Richard Attenborough) first sees the house she sighs: 'What wouldn't I give to grow old in a place like that', and one wonders how many other day trippers to the village have said the same since. The Montgomery family still own the house, and Mrs Elizabeth Montgomery (who came to both David and Nina's wedding and David's funeral) lived there until a few years ago.

Some time after the film crew left, a stone was placed over David's grave, with a short inscription:

In loving memory of
Sqn/Ldr David J.H. Maltby D.S.O. D.F.C.
R.A.F.V.R. Bomber Command
Aged 23
And of his crew
Sept. 15th 1943

The men who gather here every September are the East Kent branch of the Aircrew Association, an ex-servicemens' association open to anyone who has served as aircrew in the RAF. In effect this means people who served in the war, as there has never been large scale recruitment into the air force since. They are from my parents' generation and, even though he was a naval man, my father would have got on fine with them, yarning away in a country pub rehearsing his wartime stories.

As a surrogate for my parents, I felt slightly awkward the day I was there. With no direct experience of my own to relate I had to fall back on my family history, which of course is what brought us all together on this particular day.

While we chatted I was reminded of the odds they faced, just to survive the war. The bulk of the RAF's casualties were in Bomber Command, where the number killed made up more than 10 per cent of the entire military casualties suffered by Britain and the Commonwealth. According to some estimates, nearly half the men who actually flew in Bomber Command were killed.

David is buried at Wickhambreaux, but the bodies of his crew were never found. However, most of them are commemorated in other places: there is a plaque remembering Flt Sgt Vivian Nicholson DFM in his local church, St Mary's in Sherburn, Co Durham; Sgt Harold Simmonds' name appears in a book of remembrance in Burgess Hill

Members of the East Kent branch of the RAF Aircrew Association, after the wreath-laying ceremony at David Maltby's grave in St. Andrew's Church, Wickhambreaux, 14 September 2007.   PHOTO: CHARLES FOSTER

in Sussex; Sgt William Hatton is on a memorial board in his old school in Wakefield; Flt Sgt Victor Hill is on the memorial in Berkeley Castle in Gloucestershire, where he had been the head gardener; and there was once a bench dedicated to Flt Sgt Antony Stone in the grounds of Winchester Cathedral, although local reports suggested recently that it seems to have been moved. All their names appear on the Commonwealth Air Forces memorial at Runnymede, dedicated to the 20,456 British and Commonwealth airmen who died in the Second World War and who have no known grave.

All eight of the men who died that day are also listed at 617

IN MEMORIAM * 33

Squadron's own memorial in Woodhall Spa. This is a large monument in the shape of a dam wall, an evocative choice perhaps, but one which gives it a somewhat brutalist look. It is carved with the names of the 204 members of 617 Squadron who died between May 1943 and the end of the war. A small stream of people, some knowledgeable, others merely curious, walk up to this every day, many looking for the famous names. The dead are listed in strict alphabetical order, just initials, surnames and decorations.

The memorial is right in the centre of Woodhall Spa. The spa town grew up in the 1830s around the village's natural well, when the fashion for taking the waters was at its height, and an elegant Victorian town developed. In its heyday it was a bustling little inland resort. It still has an air of faded grandeur, little changed in decades. The Petwood Hotel is probably the town's most famous landmark, and trades heavily on its RAF connections. During the war it was requisitioned for service use and a number of squadrons – including David's first unit 97 Squadron and 617 Squadron after the Dams Raid – used it as their officers' mess. The half-timbered exterior features in many a snapshot.

Just as I was taken aback when told of the number of boys from David's school killed in the war, the six panels of names in Woodhall made me pause when I visited the memorial. So many names, so many young men, from all parts of Britain, Ireland and the Commonwealth. I searched for the names of David's crew, and took a photograph of each, but as I did so I was conscious of those listed above and below, all united first by the alphabetical proximity of their surnames but also because they had volunteered for the RAF and ended up in the same squadron.

War memorials are such a common feature in our cities, towns and villages that we scarcely notice them and frequently pass them by. I'm sure that every village in Kent has one – in Wickhambreaux there is a medium-size cross very close to David's grave. His name appears here again, among the other people from the parish who died on active service in the Second World War: The roll call of names couldn't sound more English: Sidney Bushell, John Cadman, Albert Friend, Peter Harmsworth, David Maltby, Norman Tucker, James Young. On every war memorial across the country there are similar lists: names linked by coincidence of geography, education, war service, employment – so various and so many that it makes their total number impossible to collate.

Back at David's graveside I thought of all these things, and, above all, I wondered why I had never been here before. Every year, strangers come to the place where my uncle, my mother's only brother, is buried. They place wreaths, and pay their respects, but why were we never brought here as children? I can only conclude that my mother would not, or could not, face up to the pain it would cause her. Perhaps this is one of the things that caused her so much anxiety towards the end of her life.

A tune buzzed round my head while I was in Wickhambreaux that warm late summer day. It was there again a few weeks later as I wrote these words and, suddenly, I know what it is. It's the last song from the film, *Oh! What a Lovely War*, sung just before the dramatic, awesome final shot, as the camera pulls away from a single white cross to reveal tens, hundreds, thousands more – row on row, filling the screen: 'And when they ask us how dangerous it was/Oh, we'll never tell them, no, we'll never tell them.'

Chapter 3

*

Before the War

E ttrick Maltby's diary throughout the 1920s tells a pretty typical story of a moderately well off, upper middle-class family, which is the life into which Audrey, David and Jean were born. It was the kind of family that automatically would have sent their sons away to a boarding preparatory school at the age of seven or eight, the difference being here that they actually lived in one.

The boarding prep school was a method of education that has almost completely vanished today, with the handful of schools that offer boarding facilities only doing so as weekly boarders. For the first two-thirds of the twentieth century things were quite different: boys came for a whole term at a time, eleven or twelve weeks away from home. Some schools would have a half-term holiday over a long week-end, but this was by no means common. Parents who lived near enough would be allowed to visit their children on occasional Sundays, usually taking them out for awkward lunches in nearby hotels. This kind of school has left its mark in many ways, most notably in literature. Many writers have recorded their days of happiness or, more likely, misery both as schoolboys or schoolmasters. They range from Evelyn Waugh and John Betjeman through to the more recent account of the Poet Laureate, Andrew Motion, whose memoir *In the Blood* captures the singular bewilderment of one small boy who couldn't quite work out why he was there.

There is one famous work which may be the most accurate description in print of this strange world:

all skools ... are nothing but kanes, lat. french, geog. hist, algy, geom, headmasters, skool dogs, skool sossages, my bro molesworth 2 and MASTERS everywhere. The only good things about skool are the BOYS wizz who are noble brave fearless etc. although you have various swots, bullies, cissies, milksops greedy guts and oiks with whom i am forced to mingle hem hem.[19]

These are the words of Nigel Molesworth, eponymous hero of the Molesworth books, four best-selling satires, starting with *Down with Skool!*, from the 1950s. The authors, Geoffrey Willans and Ronald Searle, were responsible for the introduction of a number of catch-phrases and sayings to the English language (like 'as any fule know'; 'hello clouds, hello sky') which people often use without knowing their provenance. Although the books are still in print, and indeed have been recently promoted to the status of Penguin Modern Classics, they are something of a cult phenomenon, reminding the nostalgic reader of a time when boys of a certain background wore grey flannel shorts all year round, learnt Latin and wrote letters home on Sundays.

Ettrick, Aileen and Audrey, then 11 months old, moved to Baldslow in May 1918, a few months before the end of the First World War. Shortly after they moved, in September, Aileen's oldest brother, Eric, was killed in France 'gallantly leading his men' from the East Kent Mounted Rifles over a hill 'swept by rifle and shell fire'. Eric was the golden boy of the Hatfeild family, the heir to the family estate at Hartsdown in Margate, and a more than useful cricketer. He had been to Eton, where he was captain of cricket, on to New College, Oxford, where he got a Blue, and then played for Kent for several seasons up to the outbreak of the war. As far as I know, he is the only relative I have who appears in *Wisden* – or on the Cricinfo website, but it was there that I discovered he was quite a respectable slow left-arm bowler, taking 64 wickets in 65 first class matches, at an average of 23.04 with a career best return of 5 for 48.

The Hatfeilds had made their money from tobacco, and were also related by marriage to other tobacco families such as the Taddys and Friends. They also had a lot of property and other interests in and around Margate. When Eric was killed, only eight years after his father had died, the estate had to pay a second large swath of death duties, so its finances were not in good order. This led to his mother, Mrs Maud Hatfeild, first selling several parcels of land and then, in 1927, Hartsdown House itself and most of its grounds, to Margate Corporation. At the same time she continued her political career,

---

19   Geoffrey Willans and Ronald Searle, *The Compleet Molesworth*, Max Parrish, 1958, p.7

Hydneye House School. Photograph taken in the 1960s, but the property would have looked much the same throughout the time the Maltby family lived there.

PHOTO: STUART ROBERTS

becoming the Corporation's first woman Mayor in 1926, and at one stage contemplating standing for parliament. She died in 1931.

The Hatfeild tobacco connections with Hartsdown weren't forgotten when the family moved out. In 1934, the Carreras company, who had taken over the Taddy family company and were the manufacturers of Black Cat cigarettes, chartered five special trains to bring 2,500 factory 'girls', on their second annual outing to Margate. A meal was served in what was described as the 'largest marquee in England' erected in Hartsdown Park. The meal was provided by 200 waiters and waitresses, and provided on 10,000 plates. Between the wars, Margate was at the height of its popularity as a resort. That year, the local press reported that more than 150,000 day trippers visited during the season.

Hydneye was a large house, and the Maltbys had both school and domestic staff, including a nanny, a maid and a cook, to help run it. This domestic support enabled Ettrick and Aileen to pursue their sporting lifestyles, especially in the school holidays. For Ettrick, this

David Maltby, at Hydneye, aged
about 2.   PHOTO: FAMILY COLLECTION

meant golf and cricket. He was a regular competitor in the famous
President's Putter competition at Rye in the first week of the New Year,
a knockout matchplay competition open to members of the Oxford and
Cambridge Society. This was made up of people who had represented
either university in the annual match between them, and contained
many of the best amateurs in the country. Although he never won the
Putter, he did secure victory in the Easter gold medal in 1929.

In the summer there was cricket. A lot of this revolved around the
Hastings Cricket Festival, the week during the summer when Sussex
County Cricket Club played their home matches in the town and sometimes even played the touring test team. Up until the 1960s cricket fes-
tivals were very popular events in seaside towns in the summer
months, attracting large crowds of trippers as well as cricket enthusi-
asts. Ettrick was elected to the committee of the County Cricket Club at
some time in the 1920s and was also on the committee that organised
the Hastings Cricket Festival. In later years, he was the Festival's
Chairman. They began a tradition of organising a cricket match
between a 'Hydneye House XI' and the Hastings Police on the Sunday
of Festival week. The series of matches lasted over 30 years, interrupted only by the war.

Aileen continued playing hockey, apparently even during the early stages of her pregnancies with both David and Jean. She played for South Saxons Hockey Club in Hastings, county matches for Sussex, regional matches for the South of England, and on several occasions for the full England team. In those days, there was often only one international match a year, usually against one of the other 'home' countries, and her first international appearance was in an away match against Ireland, scheduled for St Patrick's Day, 17 March 1923. Ettrick recorded in his diary that he saw her off on the boat train to Dublin.

At the time, there was a certain amount of apprehension about an English team going to Ireland, which was still embroiled in a bloody civil war after the formation of the Irish Free State in 1922. A boxing world title fight was also being held in Dublin on the same night but Republican plans to blow up the theatre in which this took place were thwarted. The hockey match attracted less attention, everything went well and England won 3:0. A newspaper report quoted in the history of the All England Women's Hockey Association says: 'Many people seemed anxious as to whether the match would be allowed, all other games having been stopped the previous day. However, everything passed off in perfect peace.'[20] Another report, in the *Irish Times*, signifies that Aileen had a quiet enough match. 'Now and then the Irish forwards broke away, but could never press home their attacks, and Mrs Maltby was never really tested in goal.'[21]

Aileen was part of the English contingent sent to the first Triennial Conference of the fledgling International Federation of Women's Hockey Associations set up in Geneva in 1930 'to nurture the highest possible standard of play for members of the new Federation.' She later played in the 'demonstration' match between England and the Rest of the World.[22] She went on to have a long career in hockey administration, serving on many committees and for a while as an England selector. Even in the 1960s, she was still going to the annual international hockey match at Wembley. England played one match there every spring, and it had become an outing for every hockey-playing girls' school in the country, who seemed to compete with each other as to who could scream the loudest. My mother usually went with Aileen but one year I was dragged along as well. A gawky teenager, I remember sitting in the back seat of the car in a traffic jam alongside coaches full of girls, blushing furiously as I saw the handwritten 'Boys Wanted!'

20 Nancy Tomkins, *The Century Makers: A History of the All England Women's Hockey Association 1895-1995*, p.102
21 *Irish Times*, 19 March 1923
22 Tomkins, *The Century Makers*, p.42

signs stuck up in the windows.

David was born on 10 May 1920 at home in Hydneye, at 8.45pm. Like many children of their generation, Audrey, David and (later) Jean were entrusted to the care of a nanny for a lot of their early lives. There is no record of the earlier person they employed but at some time between David and Jean being born Raynes Cook joined the family as their nanny. Ettrick notes the date of her leaving in April 1937, when Jean was 12. After that she went on to work for another family in Kent, and then retired to Bournemouth. My family got to know her well through her visits to us every summer when we lived in Plymouth. Then, soon after we moved to Gerrards Cross in 1958, she came to live with us permanently and stayed until she died in 1964. By then she was well into her 80s and, because she suffered from dementia, couldn't live on her own any more. We were always told that she had no family of her own, which is why she had come to live with us, but after she died my mother informed me that Nanny had once had a child and had to give it up for adoption, because she wasn't married. The name 'Mrs Cook', by which she was known, was a 'courtesy' title, taken up by her when she started nannying. It now seems a very matter of fact way of dealing with what must have been a very difficult time of her life.

A nanny who stayed with one family so long had a huge impact on children from this kind of background. From soon after they were born until they went away to school, she would have been the person they saw the most – getting them up and dressed in the mornings, feeding and amusing them during the day, then presenting them ready for inspection and a little quality time with their mother and father between tea and supper. Even when they went on holidays, in the case of the Maltbys camping all over Britain and Ireland, Nanny came too, and had to sleep in a tent with the youngest children.

The Maltbys were great campers and went on holidays every summer, often with relatives. Aileen's sister Mildred, and her family, the Bartlets, and Ettrick's sister Kyria, and her family, the Yules, were regular companions. Aileen and Mildred themselves built a caravan on a lorry chassis, helped by a man who worked at Hydneye who Frances Bonsey (née Bartlet) remembers was just called 'Sergeant Major'.

Nearly 80 years later Ruth Walton (née Yule) also remembers these holidays, and was able to send me some pictures taken at the time. One of them again stopped me in my tracks, and the handwritten caption

Playing at Camber Sands, June 1929. Left to right: Alan Pegler, Jean Maltby, David Maltby, David Yule.   PHOTO: RUTH WALTON

sent me off on yet another piece of research.

It is the only picture I have ever seen of David and Jean together, taken on Camber Sands in Sussex when David was 9 and Jean only 4. You can see the delight in her face, being allowed to play with the much bigger boys. It is obvious to me now that, at least at that age, she adored her older brother. You don't have to be much of an amateur psychologist to work out that this state of affairs continued for the next 14 or so years, until he was killed.

The caption told me that the other boys in the picture were David and Jean's cousin, David Yule, and a boy called Alan Pegler. I knew the latter name immediately. While we were growing up, it would crop up now and again in the news, and my mother would tell us that Alan had been a pupil at Hydneye, and been a good friend of the Maltby family.

The reason why Alan Pegler was newsworthy was because throughout the 1960s and 70s he was involved in several schemes to buy the Flying Scotsman steam locomotive, both to save it from the scrapyard and keep it running. He was always described in the press as a 'successful businessman', which indeed he was, but first and foremost he was, and still is, what is usually called a 'railway enthusiast'.

When I tracked Alan Pegler down in London, early in 2008, he still had vivid memories of his time at Hydneye and his friendship with the

Oiling the level crossing gate near Barnby Moor and Sutton station on the East Coast Main Line. David Maltby looks on as one of the railwaymen explains the procedure.

PHOTO: ALAN PEGLER

Maltbys. Even better, he had another photograph, taken when David had come to stay with his own family one summer holiday, probably when they were both 12.

Most of Alan's pictures have been lost or destroyed, but he has one album of his own photographs. At the time, he lived in north Nottinghamshire, close to the East Coast main line, and took many pictures of steam engines, signal boxes and other bits and pieces of railway paraphernalia. Amongst these is a picture of David, looking on reasonably attentively, as a railway worker lies prone on the ground reaching under a level crossing gate to oil it. 'Was David keen on railways?' I asked. 'Not really,' Alan replied, 'but he wasn't disinterested. He was quite intrigued seeing all these famous trains roaring past.'

We sometimes forget how serious childhood illnesses, such as scarlet fever and whooping cough, were in those days before vaccinations and antibiotics. Of the Maltby children, David seems to have been the worst affected, with Ettrick's diary saying he was 'pretty bad' on a couple of occasions before he was three. However, he survived, and was ready to start being formally schooled two days before his eighth birthday, at Hydneye. Two years later, in September 1930, they decided to move him on to another school, and he was sent to St Wilfrid's in nearby Hawkhurst.

The two Davids. Left, David Maltby, right, David Yule, his first cousin. Sitting on the steps at Hydneye, probably in 1929, about the same time as the Camber Sands picture on p. 41

PHOTO: RUTH WALTON

David was nearly 14 when he went away to Marlborough College. In fact he was only there for just over two years: from the start of the summer term in April 1934 to the end of the summer term in July 1936. The college's archivist, Terry Rogers, helped me trace his record by digging out old class lists and even his house rugby logbook. This indicates that he did not seem to have the sporting ability of his parents, playing only in a house second team, mainly as a second row forward: 'Maltby was slow but hard working and lasted right through the game. He was more often up with the ball than one would expect.' (In the same house and on the same team was a boy called Lionel Queripel, who was later to win the VC at Arnhem when, wounded, he stayed at his post armed with grenades and a pistol to cover the withdrawal of his troops.) David's academic achievements were about as undistinguished as those in sport, showing that he finished in the bottom half of the class most of the time.

When David left Marlborough he seems to have drifted about for a while, but then went to a school at Glen Arun near Arundel to sit his Oxford Certificate, which was an exam roughly equivalent to a modern AS level. ('David through everything except French', Ettrick records in January 1937.) By the spring of 1938, he had decided to start training as a mining engineer, a career that seems an odd choice for a 18 year old, even one who had dropped out of Marlborough. What brought him to this decision no one now seems to know.

In April Aileen and Ettrick together drove him up to Harness Grove near Worksop. Then they spent one day going 'round pits' in South Yorkshire. This was obviously some form of reconnaissance expedition trying to sort out where David should go and with whom he could stay. Harness Grove was a country house and estate associated with the Jones family, who were the owners of Rother Vale Collieries, but I have not been able to establish whether either Ettrick or Aileen actually knew them. However, it is in the part of Nottinghamshire from which Ettrick's family came, so it is possible that there was some connection. Farndon, where Ettrick's grandfather had been the Rector for many years, is less than 30 miles away, and Southwell Minster has a window dedicated to the Maltby family. Ettrick and Aileen mixed up this trip with a little holiday, staying at Forest Lodge near Retford and Ettrick spent three or four days playing golf at Firbeck and Lindrick.

By 24 October 1938 everything seemed to have been sorted out. Using a phrase that crops up several times in his diary, obviously a favourite of his, he wrote 'David left home to start his new life at Treeton.' Aileen went with him, as Ettrick obviously had to stay at the school. Treeton is a small village in South Yorkshire, roughly halfway between Sheffield and Rotherham. Although it is a historic village, mentioned in the Domesday Book, by the early 20th century it was dominated by the colliery, which was the major industry in the area. In 1938 more than 1,000 men worked below ground at the pit, with nearly 300 more at the surface. The colliery, along with the nearby Fence and Orgreave mines, was owned by Rother Vale Collieries, and then by its successor, United Steel Companies.

Most of the information that I have now about David's year in Yorkshire is gleaned from the obituaries published after his death. In September 1943, the *Isle of Thanet Gazette* recorded that David 'began at the bottom of the ladder by working in the pit and lodging with a miner's family. His gift for making friends in all walks of life made him most popular with the miners and their families.' The lodgings appear to have been with a family called Smith in nearby Aughton, since Ettrick records that they visited him there on 3 January 1939, after he had been home for Christmas 1938. By April that year, David could obviously afford to run a car of his own, since Ettrick drove it to Forest Lodge and met him there.

Life at Hydneye may have been relatively well-appointed but by the time I remember their visits, in the 1960s, Ettrick and Aileen had downsized a little. However their old fashioned speech patterns ('orf' for 'off', 'Marmeet' for 'Marmite') still remained, the kind endlessly parodied since by the likes of Harry Enfield. In my grandparents' world, people didn't drive, they motored, they wore Aertex shirts, sat on tartan picnic rugs and smoked endless packs of Player's. Gentlemen played cricket as amateurs and joined the services as officers.

If all this sounds like an idealised vision of a 'Betjemanesque' golden age, furnished and burnished by the sun, then perhaps it was. Having a boys' prep school with its many bedrooms and acres of grounds as your house may have given Ettrick a taste for a grander style of living than he probably could afford. In what could almost be seen as a caricature from Molesworth, he always had an abiding interest in what had won the 3.30 at Sandown, and by 1938, his diary records that he had taken on an accountant 'to straighten things out'. This led to a lot of tension 'behind the green-baize door', as my mother elliptically called what I assume to be the private areas of the school. She always said that Ettrick lost any money he made from running the school, and plenty more of Aileen's inheritance from the Hatfeilds as well. In the end, Aileen took firm control of their financial arrangements, and he seems to have accepted that.

Whatever stability they had reached was about to be shaken severely. On 4 August 1939, they had gone to Harness Grove to spend their summer holiday camping. They drove over to Treeton to see David, and Ettrick recorded that he went down a mine on 9 August. On 22 August, they travelled by river from Worksop to Farndon. However, they must have been keeping in touch with the news since in what looks like a change of plan, Ettrick wrote on 25 August: 'Decided to pack up & leave Harness Grove next morning.' By Friday 1 September, they were back at home. Ettrick drove over to Horsham to fetch a puppy, and while he was there he heard that Hitler had invaded Poland. The car broke down on their way home; not a good sign. On the Sunday, Neville Chamberlain made his historic broadcast announcing that war had been declared, and on Monday 4 September 1939 David gave up his mining career, and came home to enlist.

Chapter 4

✳

Training

When the war started David must have decided that he wanted to join the RAF – but then so did tens of thousands of
other young men. Most of them (including David) were told
to go away and wait, and that they would be invited for assessment as
soon as possible. In David's case this didn't happen until 20 March
1940, when, as his service record shows, he formally joined the RAF
Volunteer Reserve and was accepted for aircrew training. Curiously,
there is no mention of this in Ettrick's diaries.

It seems a little strange that, in wartime, people were still being
recruited into what sounds more like a peacetime body, a 'Volunteer
Reserve'. In fact the RAFVR had been set up in 1936 as part of the wave
of pre-war rearmament. For some reason, the Air Ministry carried on
using the RAFVR as the mechanism for joining up new recruits
throughout the war, and by its end in 1945 nearly all the surviving RAF
aircrew (as opposed to those from the Commonwealth air forces) had
joined in this way.

At his assessment in March David would have undergone an interview and a medical examination to see whether he was suitable for
flying. The young men who passed were then given a silver badge –
and then sent home again, to wait a little while longer. Another delay of
three or four months was perfectly normal.

However, at this time the Maltby family was in a state of upheaval. It
was now fairly obvious that anywhere on the south-east coast of
England was not a safe place for a boys' school because of the possibility of invasion. In any case they weren't going to be allowed to stay at
Hydneye because the army informed them in early May that the building and grounds were to be requisitioned. So Aileen drove down to the
West Country on 18 May to search for a place to which they could evacu-
ate the school, and David went with her. They looked at houses in

Devon and Somerset and settled on Witherdon Manor, a large house in Germansweek in Devon, a country village roughly halfway between Holsworthy and Okehampton.

By Thursday 23 May, they decided to go: vans were ordered, letters sent to all the parents, and various relatives arrived to help with the packing. Although she was still at boarding school, the Beehive in Shropshire, Jean was brought back for a fortnight to lend a hand. Two vans were dispatched the next day, and on 25 May Aileen, Jean, Ettrick's sister Kyria Yule and her husband Charles, and two unnamed 'Frognall maids' set off. Crowds of parents arrived – probably more of a hindrance than a help – and a boy called Hargreaves broke his wrist. 'A terrible day and night', Ettrick wrote in his diary. The following day, a Sunday, the main convoy set off. A total of 75 family members, boys and staff left at 8.20 am to drive the 230 miles in a fleet of buses, cars and vans, arriving in Devon at 7.50 that evening.

David and Aileen made two further trips back to Hastings in the next two weeks bringing a van and a truck down to Devon, along with whatever else they could pack in, including Mr and Mrs Tinson, a couple who worked at Hydneye as an odd job man and a maid. On 10 June, the day Italy joined the war, the whole school was taken to Bude to go swimming, perhaps to keep the boys out of the way. By 14 June, some sort of order was restored and Ettrick was able to write: 'Fall of Paris. All staff settled at Lodges.'

In the middle of all this domestic chaos, on 6 June, David at last received his call-up papers. He was given a fortnight's notice to present himself at the RAF Receiving Unit at Uxbridge on Thursday 20 June, when he would begin aircrew training as a member of the RAF Volunteer Reserve. Like all RAFVR recruits, David joined at the lowest rank, an Aircraftman. There had been no officer entry into the Volunteer Reserve since it had first been established in 1936. As the Air Council explained at the time, in a report quoted by historian John Terraine, the new force was to be open:

> to the whole middle class in the widest sense of the term, namely, the complete range of the output of the public and secondary schools... In a force so recruited, it would be inappropriate to grade the members on entry as officers or airmen according to their social class; entry will accordingly be on a common footing, as airman pilot or observer, and

promotion to commissioned rank will be made at a later stage in accordance with the abilities for leadership actually displayed.[23]

The RAF may have been relatively classless, but there was still the expectation in its upper echelons that privately educated boys made the best officers (and pilots) while the state sector would produce the observers (at that stage the only other people who flew) and the tradesmen with the specialist skills needed for groundcrew. In mid 1940, the operational heavy bomber with its seven- or eight-man crew was still a year and a half away. It would provide many more chances for NCOs to fly – mainly as gunners, a job almost exclusively filled by 'ordinary' people, according to one account.[24]

A couple of years at Marlborough, not to mention 18 months training as a mining engineer, might have earmarked David as potential officer and pilot material, but before he could reach that pinnacle he had to face a year or more of training, moving in stages through an almost baffling series of initials. The ITW, AFS, OTU and HCU were amongst the delights that awaited the young trainees.

David's first posting was back in Devon. Three days after joining up, he was transferred to No 4 Initial Training Wing (ITW) in Paignton. This was housed in the grand surroundings of Oldway Mansion, a country house built for the Singer sewing machine family in the 1870s, in the style of the Palace of Versailles. The ITW course lasted for about twelve weeks, and involved a mixture of drill, PT and parachute training as well as classroom instruction on such matters as armaments, aircraft recognition, hygiene and meteorology. At the same time, men who had been selected as possible pilots ('pilots under training') would start some classes in aerodynamics and the principles of flying.

On 19 August, David was sent to Elementary Flying Training School, at Ansty in Warwickshire, receiving one to one instruction in the famous old training aircraft, the Tiger Moth. After about 15 hours instruction, the student was supposed to be able to 'go solo', a process which involved taking the aeroplane up into the air solo, flying to 1,000 ft, doing a mile square around the airfield, and landing. On 6 September, he was nearly bumped off the course 'on spinning', but was allowed to continue. With an air of delight, Ettrick recorded that he had managed his first solo flight on 13 September 'after being very nearly turned down!'

---

23 Terraine, *The Right of the Line*, p.43
24 James Taylor and Martin Davidson, *Bomber Crew*, Hodder & Stoughton, 2005, p.109

Flying an elderly biplane is one thing, becoming a battle-ready pilot needed more training on more advanced aircraft. The first phase of this took place at a Service Flying Training School. David was sent to No 12 SFTS at RAF Grantham (later called RAF Spitalgate to distinguish it from the headquarters of No 5 Bomber Command Group who were also housed in the town, at a large house called St Vincents). While David was there most of the training was being done on twin-engine Avro Anson aircraft. These were no longer used in front line service but continued to be produced in large numbers throughout the war because of their role as a trainer.

The training was now a lot more advanced and took in much more complex manoeuvres. Pilots learned about flying at night, in formation and the basics of techniques such as corkscrewing to escape from fighter attack. This was the most drastic thing that a pilot could do, and involved banking one way using full rudder, diving 1,000 ft, wrenching the ailerons the other way, climbing again, turning the other way, and diving again. And repeat, hoping that the fighter had lost your tail, or that your rear gunner could get a bead on it. Hard enough to do in a twin-engine Anson, weighing 4 tons, bloody terrifying in a 30 ton Lancaster. It was pretty intense – David had only one period of leave at the beginning of September, and training went on through Christmas, so he didn't even get home.(His first formation flight was on 27 December 1940.) But by 18 January he had finished, almost exactly seven months after turning up at RAF Uxbridge. He was a qualified pilot and was awarded his wings.

The day he got his wings he was promoted to Sergeant. The very next day he was given a commission and thereby became an officer. About two-thirds of newly qualified pilots were made officers, although it was never defined exactly what were the 'officer-like qualities' that distinguished them from their brother pilots. Some officers did not have middle-class backgrounds or public-school education, but if you did it was certainly seen as an asset.

The RAF's promotion policy also meant that all NCO aircrew had at least to be given the rank of sergeant. This led to the situation which became common later in the war where an 18 year old air gunner with only a few months training was senior to middle-aged groundcrew with several years experience.

David had two more training stints to go through before he was ready to fly on operations – air navigation school and an operational training unit. The first of these was in Cranage, Cheshire, home of the No. 1 School of Air Navigation. A number of other newly qualified pilots were on the same course, among them Sgt John (Tommy) Thompson, who had also just left a Service Flying Training School, in his case No. 14 SFTS at Cranfield, Bedfordshire. I was able to trace Tommy from a posting he had left on a Dambusters website (how did writers do their research before the arrival of the internet?) and he told me his story.

The Cranage course was meant to give bomber pilots specialist navigating skills, so it concentrated on plotting, meteorology, star sight navigation and signals. They flew Ansons, learning to navigate them all over northern England. On the course there was no differentiation between the sergeant pilots and the commissioned pilot officers, with all the trainees billeted in the same wooden huts, which Tommy remembers as 'quite comfortable'. For an evening out they would travel into Northwich and visit the pubs there. Nearly everyone asked to describe David says he was 'tall and quiet', and Tommy is no exception. But the two young pilots became quite close friends and shared a trip south on a leave weekend:

> About half way through the course we had a weekend leave and managed to scrounge enough petrol coupons to drive us both down to my home in Havant and for him to catch the train on to Worthing on the Friday. He arrived back on the Sunday and we drove back to Cranage. Road sign-posts had been removed in case of a German invasion and it was a good job we were fairly expert navigators equipped with current Quarter Million charts from the school. I was glad to have him to read the maps and discuss nav problems on a dark country route.[25]

This presents a slight mystery as exactly where David went on this weekend leave, which was probably in February 1941. Tommy is sure, 66 years later, that David told him he was going to Worthing. He certainly didn't go to Devon, because Ettrick wrote in his diary in March that he came back on leave for the first time since September 1940, and by that time he had left Cranage.

David and Tommy both passed the navigation course in March, and were then sent on the final posting of their pre-operational training, to

25   John (Tommy) Thompson, Email to author, 6 April 2007

No. 16 Operational Training Unit in Upper Heyford, Oxfordshire. Tommy's car came in useful again, as he took both of them and their kit down to the new base, which again had reasonably comfortable accommodation in two country houses nearby. At first they flew Ansons, but moved on to the Handley Page Hampden later on. The Hampden, a twin-engine medium bomber with a crew of four, had been in service since the mid 1930s. It was, along with the Wellington, the mainstay of the bomber fleet.

At this stage Tommy and David's paths parted: Tommy was taken off the heavy bomber course after only getting 80% in his exams (he was eventually posted to another OTU flying Blenheim light bombers and went on to a Blenheim squadron), but David stayed on, learning to fly with a crew, and building up the necessary team skills that they might need when on real-life operations. There were lessons, and examinations, in such subjects as parachuting, dinghy drill, aircraft layout, fuel systems, low-level flying, bombing and gunnery, with target practice.[26]

David then acquired his own car and one weekend was able to 'motor down from Oxford' (Ettrick's words) to Witherdon to inspect the craters left by a salvo of 15 bombs that had fallen from an errant German bomber a few days before. The trainee bomber pilot's expert opinion was obviously useful here.

David's last couple of months at OTU seem to have passed without much incident. He celebrated his 21st birthday on Saturday 10 May. On his previous birthday he was still waiting for his call-up for aircrew training, and it was still less than nine months since he had first piloted a Tiger Moth, circling around an airfield in Warwickshire. Now he was ready to fly a bomber, and to go to war.

26 Taylor and Davidson, *Bomber Crew*, p.112

Chapter 5

Nos 106 and 97 Squadrons

D uring the Second World War the flat countryside around the city of Lincoln was home to many Bomber Command airfields, mainly operated by the squadrons in the Command's No 5 Group. There were about twelve squadrons in the group in 1942, but the number varied from month to month as they were formed, amalgamated or disbanded. David's first posting as an operational pilot in June 1941 was to 106 Squadron at RAF Coningsby in Lincolnshire, the same airfield from which he would take off two and a quarter years later on his final flight.

David had just been home on a week's leave and was seen off at the railway station by both Ettrick and Aileen. When he arrived at Coningsby on Thursday 5 June he found out that he was just a few miles away from some family friends, Bettie and Woodroffe Walter, in nearby Woodhall Spa. Woodroffe (always known as Woody) was a local estate agent and auctioneer, and they lived in a large house near the centre of the town, called Kenilworth.

The Hampdens that David had flown at the Operational Training Unit were gradually being replaced by the first of the heavy bombers: the Avro Manchester. This had a crew of six or seven, but only two Rolls Royce Vulture engines, which were prone to failure. The Manchester had come into service in January 1941 but within a few months of starting operations it suffered repeated groundings while modifications were carried out. The decision was then made to fit the same airframe with four engines, and change these from the Vultures to the more reliable Merlins, also made by Rolls Royce. So the famous Lancaster aircraft was born.

David arrived in the middle of this period of uncertainty. Within a fortnight he would be flying the unreliable Manchester, but his first five operations were in Hampdens. So after just three short training flights, he was off on his first operation, on Wednesday 11 June 1941, bombing Duisburg in the Ruhr Valley. His crew were Plt Off Campbell, Sgt Bishop and Sgt Edwards. The time for the flight to Duisburg and back was over six hours and was hardly the short easy operation on which new crews were traditionally sent. The 106 Squadron Operations Record Book gives the bald details: 'Bombed from 15,000ft. Owing to 10/10ths cloud, results not observed but estimated to fall near a large red fire.'

However, like many bombing raids at this time, it may not have been very effective. In their detailed analysis of every single raid of the war, the *Bomber Command War Diaries,* published some 40 years later, Martin Middlebrook and Chris Everitt describe it thus:

> 80 aircraft – 36 Whitleys, 35 Hampdens, 9 Halifaxes. 8/10ths cloud over target but good bombing reported. 1 Whitley lost. There are no reports from the two main targets but Cologne reports bombs from aircraft which were either mistaking Cologne for the correct target or using it as an alternative. The main railway station was hit by 7 bombs and much damage was caused. Dock areas, a wagon works and 173 houses were also damaged. 14 people were killed and 36 injured. Because of its position just outside the main defences and industrial haze of the Ruhr, Cologne was always likely to be attacked in this way.[27]

David would not have known it but by mid 1941 there were serious worries in the upper reaches of the Government about how well the bombers were doing their job. So much so that Lord Cherwell, Churchill's personal scientific adviser and a powerful figure behind the scenes in Downing Street, asked Mr D M Butt of the War Cabinet Secretariat to analyse photographs taken by bombing crews as they reached their targets during that June and July. Butt spent the early part of August 1941 on his research, and the results were both astonishing and deeply depressing. Overall only one-third of the bombs dropped were landing within five miles of the aiming point, and in the Ruhr the proportion dropped to one-tenth.

To senior RAF commanders, Butt's report was hardly news. They already suspected that dropping relatively small bombs from high altitude was not doing serious damage. But it was a revelation to one per-

---

27 Martin Middlebrook and Chris Everitt, *Bomber Command War Diaries,* Midland Publishing, 1996, p.160

son – Churchill. The Prime Minister was furious, demanding that the Chief of the Air Staff take immediate action. The card of the C-in-C of Bomber Command, Air Marshal Sir Richard Peirse, was marked although it would be a few more months before he finally departed.

Young Pilot Officers like David would hardly have known what was going on at Bomber Command Headquarters in High Wycombe, let alone in Downing Street and Whitehall. They were at the sharp end and their priorities were navigating to the target safely, dropping their bombs as accurately as possible, and then returning home. David completed four more trips in June, in three of them bombing from 15,000 ft and reporting that his bombs fell in the target area. His final flight in 106 Squadron came on 24 June when, having set off to attack Kiel, he had to turn back with engine failure and jettisoned his bombs in the sea.

The very next day, David was transferred to 97 Squadron. Both 106 and 97 Squadrons were based at Coningsby and shared the same facilities, so he didn't have to pack his kit. It seems that he was scheduled to fly one of 97 Squadron's Manchesters and indeed he certainly had at least one practice flight in one. But on 1 July Bomber Command HQ decided it had to do something about the aircraft's persistent mechanical failures and stopped all Manchester operations. Three days later, after yet another crash on a training flight, they were grounded completely. Some 97 Squadron crews carried on operating with the 106 Squadron Hampdens but David was sent on leave.

No. 97 Squadron was one of the RAF's newer squadrons, although there had been several earlier squadrons bearing the same number, going back to December 1917. In early 1941, a large donation was made to the war effort by the government of what were then called the 'Straits Settlements'. This was a British colony made up of the provinces of Singapore, Penang and Malacca on the Malay peninsula, all of which are now in Malaysia. Within 12 months the people of the Settlements were the brutalised victims of Japan's sudden entry into the war. The money they supplied was used to pay for several Avro Manchester aircraft and when it was re-formed in February 1941 the new squadron was named 97 (Straits Settlements) Squadron in the colony's honour.

After a week back in Devon, David returned to find that 97 Squadron had now been given Hampdens of its own. The Squadron was reorganised into two Flights, with A Flight flying Hampdens and B

David Maltby at the controls of an Avro Manchester, the unloved and unreliable precursor of the Lancaster. Probably taken in the autumn of 1941.

Flight on Manchesters. David was placed in A Flight, which was commanded by Sqn Ldr 'Flap' Sherwood (who would later win a DSO after being shot down on the Augsburg Raid). Between 6 and 18 August he was to fly on six operations, five of them with the same crew: Sgt Bedell, Flt Sgt Elcoat and Sgt LW Jones. Sgt Ferguson replaced Sgt Jones on the sixth.

On Monday 18 August David flew a Hampden on a raid for the last time, as part of the last operation carried out by 97 Squadron in Hampdens. There would be no more operations until October. A concerted effort was to be made to get the heavy bombers up and running, so the squadron was reorganised again, with A Flight becoming a Manchester training flight. The Air Ministry knew by then that the Lancaster had gone into production, and would eventually replace the Manchester, although it would be several more months before deliveries would reach squadrons.

In fact, Bomber Command was to go on operating with its medium bomber fleet until well into 1942. On the first Thousand Bomber Raid in May 1942, when nearly every operational aircraft was pressed into flying, there were no fewer than 602 of the venerable twin-engine Wellingtons, which had entered service in 1938. By contrast there were only 73 Lancasters (and 79 Hampdens).[28]

David had a couple of periods home on leave while his Manchester training was going on, and on the second he brought his new girl-friend, Georgina (always known as Nina) Goodson, along with him. 'D came on leave bringing Nina with him – for first time', wrote Ettrick on 13 October. This was to be the first of several trips the couple were to make to Devon before they got married in May 1942. Nina had been living with her sister Bettie in Woodhall Spa. Although the Goodson/Walter and Maltby families had known each other for a while, and Bettie and Woody's son Richard was at school at Hydneye, it would seem that it was sometime in the late summer of 1941 that they first started going out.

When it first came into service the Manchester had a crew of six. Four of these had specialist roles – an observer (a trained navigator), who also aimed the bombs and manned the front gun turret, two wireless operator/air gunners, one of whom operated the mid-upper turret and a rear gunner. However, it still carried two qualified pilots. One was supposed to be an experienced second tour man, the second someone recently out of a Hampden OTU. So when 97 Squadron went back on ops in October David was flying as 2nd Pilot, alongside the more experienced Flt Lt Elmer Coton, who had already flown a full tour in 144 Squadron. They flew three operations in October, one to Kiel and two to Hamburg. On 7 November they were to fly together for the last time, on the night when Bomber Command put together a record effort and dispatched 392 aircraft to fly to Germany. This was an important day in Bomber Command as the raid was to prove Air Marshal Sir Richard Peirse's downfall. Already weakened by the criticism that had followed the Butt report, Peirse was probably frustrated by a long run of bad weather and poor bombing results so decided to mount a major effort on this night, with Berlin as the main target. His real problem came with his stubbornness:

> He persisted in this decision despite a late weather forecast that showed there would be a large area of bad weather with storms, thick cloud,

28 Middlebrook and Everitt, *Bomber Command War Diaries*, p.272

icing and hail over the North Sea routes by which the bombers would need to fly to Berlin and back. Air Vice Marshal Slessor of 5 Group [which included 97 Squadron] objected to the plan and was allowed to withdraw his part of the Berlin force and send it to Cologne instead.[29]

Slessor's objections probably saved many lives that night, since 21 of the 169 aircraft that went to Berlin did not return, a shocking 12 per cent of the force. (All 75 aircraft that went to Cologne returned.) What made things worse was Peirse's efforts to shift the blame. At first he said that the meteorologists had not given him sufficient warning of the worsening conditions and also that a number of pilots were not well enough trained in long-distance flying. However his boss, the Chief of the Air Staff, Air Chief Marshal Sir Charles Portal was not convinced when he found out that, on the day, the weather forecasters had predicted very severe conditions as early as 1600, well before the scheduled take off time. Also, it was felt that if the crews were insufficiently trained the onus was on their commanders to train them properly rather than send them out unprepared. Peirse was summoned to Chequers for an uncomfortable meeting with Churchill. In January 1942, he was finally shoved off to the Far East, where he served for a couple more years until he caused a further major sensation, and ended his career, by running off with the wife of Field Marshal Claude Auchinleck.

On 13 November the Air Ministry decided to cut back on the number of operations being flown against Germany especially in bad weather. The War Cabinet had decided that it was necessary to conserve resources 'in order to build a strong force to be available by the spring of next year'.[30]

The spring of 1942, for which the air marshals were delaying, promised not only better weather and the first substantial deliveries of four-engine bombers from the factories, but above all the means to navigate with improved accuracy over Germany. The scientists had devised a radio-pulse system codenamed Gee, by which the navigator of an aircraft could fix his position by reference to three transmitting stations in England.[31]

Back at 97 Squadron, the training on Manchesters carried on, dur-

29 Middlebrook and Everitt, *Bomber Command War Diaries*, p.217
30 Directive quoted in Hastings, *Bomber Command*, p.126
31 Hastings, *Bomber Command*, p.127

ing which time David qualified as 1st Pilot and got a crew of his own. Although the Squadron carried out a few low-key operations, David did not participate. He, and his new crew, would not fly on any operations until the New Year, and when they did, it would be their last flight in the unloved Manchester aircraft.

In acknowledgement of David and Nina's status as a couple, Ettrick and Aileen went up to Woodhall Spa for Christmas and stayed with Bettie and Woody until the New Year. Nina's parents George and Hilda Goodson were also there, as well as Jean, Audrey and her husband Johnnie, back on leave from the army. Ettrick records that they were all together on Christmas Day, and that he spent Boxing Day playing golf with Woody, George and Johnnie, and then went to a dance at the Petwood Hotel, which had been requisitioned by the RAF as an Officers Mess. David would later stay in the Petwood when he was moved to the new base outside the town.

The first Lancasters to go into service had been delivered to 44 Squadron at RAF Waddington on Christmas Eve. No. 97 Squadron was next in line for the new aircraft and the first arrived on 14 January 1942. Even to those who had already flown Manchesters, the Lancaster must have been an impressive sight. To those who had only flown Hampdens or Wellingtons it must have seemed like a giant. It was only a foot or so longer than the Hampden, but it was nearly 5 ft taller, and when fully loaded weighed three times as much. Even more impressive was the amount of weaponry it could carry with its four Merlin engines: 14,000 lb of bombs with enough fuel for a 1,600 mile round trip. Thus it could reach well into the eastern part of Germany, and even as far as northern Italy.

The arrival of operational Lancasters at two airfields coincided almost exactly with the most important change in personnel at the top of Bomber Command. Air Marshal Sir Arthur Harris arrived in High Wycombe as the new C-in-C. Known as Bert to his friends, Butch to his crews and Bomber to the general public, Harris was to spend the rest of the war in this job. As Max Hastings points out, the bomber war had scarcely begun when Harris took over. This would soon change and his name would be indelibly linked with its fortunes. 'There are a lot of people who say that bombing cannot win the war,' he told a newsreel interviewer. 'My reply is that it has never been tried yet. We shall see.'[32] Harris also approved changes in aircrew training and designations

32 Hastings, *Bomber Command*, pp. 134-5

which had just been proposed. Specialist navigators and air bombers were given their own designation, rather than all being lumped together as 'observers', and the roles of air gunners and wireless operators were also separated. In an emergency, wireless operators might man guns but gunners themselves were no longer required to take a wireless course. The changes also included the dropping of the necessity for a 2nd pilot on heavy bombers. It was decided that a lot of the duties he performed while airborne could be handled by a specialist engineer. There were plenty of skilled engineers in groundcrew who could be induced to fly, the thinking went, and they would take less time to train than pilots. However, it took a while for all these changes to permeate through: David had a 2nd pilot, usually George Lancey, in the seat beside him for the whole of the rest of his first tour of operations. But by July 1942, when his crew moved on, and George Lancey became a 1st pilot, they acquired a flight engineer, a Sgt Neary.

It had been the case for a while that anyone who flew should have the rank of at least sergeant, but at about this time the arrival of these larger crews led the Canadians to push for all aircrew to be commissioned. It wasn't at all uncommon for the 'captain' of a bomber crew, the pilot, to be an NCO while an officer, nominally senior to him, flew as a gunner, bomb aimer or navigator. At an air training conference in Ottawa in May 1942, the RCAF, coming from a young country with more egalitarian principles, thought this was unfair, and said so. However, the RAF would have none of this:

> A commission is granted in recognition of character, intelligence (as distinct from academic qualifications), and capacity to lead, command and set a worthy example. Many aircrews, though quite capable of performing their duties adequately, have no officer qualities. The policy proposed by Canada would have the effect of depreciating the value of commissioned rank.[31]

Even in the middle of a war the services could find time to defend the class basis of their decision, although as John Terraine says, they could hardly be blamed for not wanting to overturn an established and working system, whatever its anomalies, at a critical moment in a war for survival.

The day after the first Lancaster for 97 Squadron arrived at

---

31 Terraine, *Right of the Line*, p.465

Coningsby, 15 January, David flew on his 17th operation, his first as the 1st pilot of a heavy bomber. This was his last operation in a Manchester, and they dropped 1,190 incendiaries over Hamburg. His crew that night was the one with which he had been training since 3 January, flying half a dozen practice flights in that time. It was made up of Sgt George Lancey (2nd pilot), Sgt Max Smith (navigator), Sgt Eric Grimwood (wireless operator), Sgt Harold Rouse (bomb aimer), and gunners Sgt Harvey Legace and Plt Off Walter Kirkwood-Hackett. Sgt Lyle Humphrey would shortly replace Kirkwood-Hackett as a gunner when they transferred to one of the new Lancasters. It was given a number on the 97 Squadron operations board – Crew No 21.

✳　✳　✳

A huge piece of luck dropped into my email inbox while I was still writing the first draft of this book. I had just made a note of the names of this crew, realising that they had flown together for most of the rest of David's tour in 97 Squadron. I had also noticed that a number of them had carried on flying together after June 1942, when his tour finished, in an aircraft now captained by the newly commissioned Plt Off G W Lancey, the Canadian who had flown as a 'second dicky' sergeant pilot with David. Then, one day idly flicking through the online version of the 617 Squadron Operations Record Book I came across a Flt Lt G W Lancey, and noticed that he had joined 617 Squadron in late 1944 and had flown in many of the squadron's operations up until the end of the war, which he appeared to have survived. Although it was probably the same person, I had decided not to waste time searching for him when I had many more pressing things to follow up.

But then, a few months later in June 2007, as I deleted the spam that had built up in my email inbox after a week away on holiday the name 'Kevin Lancey' appeared. It was a message from the son of George Lancey: he had contacted Kevin Bending of the 97 Squadron Association, and been passed on to me. Kevin Lancey had quite a lot of material that his now deceased father had brought back from the war, including several photographs and an invitation to David and Nina's wedding, which apparently he and the rest of the crew had attended! Would I like to see it? When he sent me the material, I realised how lucky I was that Kevin had contacted me. Here was a picture of David

David Maltby with his crew in 97 Squadron, 'Crew No 21'. Standing left to right: Sgt Max Smith, Sgt Lyle (Pop) Humphrey, Sgt Harold Rouse, Flg Off David Maltby (pilot), Sgt Eric (Grim) Grimwood, Sgt Harvey (Leg) Legace. In hatch, Sgt George Lancey (2nd pilot). The aircraft they are standing beside was Avro Manchester L7474 in which they only flew on two separate days, 3 and 8 January 1942, so it is likely that the photograph was taken on one of those two days.   PHOTO: KEVIN LANCEY

that I don't think anyone in Britain has ever seen, photographed with the first heavy-bomber crew he had ever captained, taken on what seems to have been a very cold and wet day, standing next to a Manchester aircraft, No. L7474. Kevin even knew all the names in the picture: Max Smith, Lyle 'Pop' Humphrey, Harold Rouse, David Maltby, Eric 'Grim' Grimwood, Harvey 'Leg' Legace and crouching in the hatch above, his father, George Lancey. Eric Grimwood was killed on an operation in July 1942, but it appears that the rest (apart from David, of course) survived the war. George Lancey stayed in touch with some of them for a while. George himself had stayed in the RCAF after he had gone back to Canada, and ended up as a Squadron Leader. Then he had gone into business, and died in the 1970s. The crew appear to have only flown the particular Manchester in the picture on two occasions, on 3 and 8 January 1942, so it is very likely that the picture was taken on one of those two days.

✻ ✻ ✻

On 18 February the newly promoted Flying Officer Maltby had his first flight in a Lancaster, flying as both 2nd pilot and 1st pilot on the same day. On 24 February he went up for his first flight with George Lancey as 2nd pilot, in a short trip for the two of them to get the hang of the new aircraft. A further month or so was taken up in training on the new machine, including a long cross country flight with a 9000 lb bomb load on 10 March. While the training was going on the squadron also moved out of Coningsby. A new satellite station at Woodhall Spa itself had just been built and 97 Squadron was to be the first to occupy it. There was a nice bonus for the officers – their mess and quarters were to be in the recently requisitioned Petwood Hotel – a handy place for socialising.

The first operation flown by 97 Squadron in Lancasters was finally flown on 20 March. Six Lancasters were sent on a mine-laying operation ('gardening' was the RAF's not very subtle code word for this) over the Frisian Islands. It wasn't a very auspicious occasion. One aircraft crash-landed near Boston soon after take-off when its wingtips broke off. Another one was badly damaged on landing, after being diverted by atrocious weather conditions to RAF Abingdon.

The wingtip problem caused something of a stir, and all the new aircraft were grounded while the problem was sorted out. It all sounded ominously like the Manchester saga. This didn't stop a visit by the King and Queen to the Avro factory in Yeadon on the day they were grounded, 20 March 1942, to see the new production going on. The problem turned out to be minor, and the Yeadon production lines worked so hard that they managed to build some 200 Lancasters between February and July 1942. One of them, signed by the Queen on her visit and given the official name 'Elizabeth', duly turned up at Woodhall for 97 Squadron use.[32] Inevitably it was nicknamed Queenie. (This aircraft ended up being the favourite of Flt Lt Joe McCarthy when he

32   Bruce Robertson, *Lancaster: The Story of a Famous Bomber*, Harleyford, 1969, p.15

The Petwood Hotel, Woodhall Spa. A modern photograph – but the outside has changed very little since it served as an Officers Mess during the war.

PHOTO: CHARLES FOSTER

arrived at 97 Squadron late in 1942. He liked its nickname so much that he used it on all the Lancasters he flew later in the war. McCarthy, an American who had travelled north to enlist in the RCAF before his own country joined the war, was to transfer to 617 Squadron with David in March 1943 and fly on Operation Chastise.)

It wasn't until 8 April that David and Crew No. 21 flew on their first Lancaster mission, 'gardening' in the 'Rosemary area', which meant minelaying in Heligoland off Germany's North Sea coast. This was the first Lancaster operation of the ten more they would fly before the end of David's tour.

On 17 April, David's crew was fortunate not to be selected to be one of the six aircraft from 97 Squadron who were part of a group of 12 Lancasters flying on a very difficult raid on the MAN diesel works in Augsburg. It was a 1,500 mile round trip with the outward run in daylight, which meant that the aircraft were much more easily detected. Only six of the twelve returned, and daylight raids were rarely used again.

Detail from the reconnaisance photograph of the Tirpitz, supplied to 97 Squadron in April 1942. The ship can clearly be seen moored tight up against the fjord wall, and protected against torpedo attack by booms in the water.

However, David and his crew were selected for the next long distance raid on another totemic target, the battleship *Tirpitz*. This had been moved to Trondheim, a fjord in the far north of Norway, which the Germans hoped was beyond bomber range. But it could be reached if aircraft took off from the north of Scotland, so it was decided to launch an attack starting from Lossiemouth and Kinloss in Morayshire. A detachment of groundcrew was sent up by train, and seven Lancasters from 97 Squadron flew to Lossiemouth. They were to meet up with more Lancasters, from 44 Squadron, and Halifaxes from 10, 35 and 76 Squadrons, who would fly from Kinloss.[33]

Throughout the war the Allied authorities were always worried that the *Tirpitz*, the sister ship of the *Bismarck*, would break out into the North Atlantic and wreak havoc amongst the convoys running between North America and Britain. With its formidable guns and top speed of over 30 knots, it was certainly well equipped to do so. Several different methods of attack were tried on a number of occasions, ranging from bombing raids to midget submarines. None of these worked, until finally, in November 1944, a joint operation by 617 and 9 Squadrons destroyed it with the massive Tallboy bombs. It can certainly be argued that preventing the *Tirpitz* ever firing a shot in anger during the entire war was a success in itself.

For the attack in which David was involved, the plan was for the Halifaxes to fly into the fjord at low level and drop mines that were meant to strike the ship below the water line, while the Lancasters bombed from above, trying to damage the superstructure and draw fire away from their comrades.

Among the material sent to me by Kevin Lancey was a reconnaissance photograph of the *Tirpitz* in its fjord, which must have been given to the crews as part of their briefing. The difficulty of the operation can be seen at once: the ship is moored hard up against the sheer side of a cliff, protected by clearly visible torpedo nets.

The aircrews all arrived in northern Scotland on 23 April, and the raid was scheduled for the next evening. But the weather intervened and on 24 April, and the following two nights, the operation was postponed. So the RAF types did what RAF types did best – throw an enormous impromptu party. On three successive nights, the crews from the five separate squadrons invaded Elgin, a quiet and respectable market town on the main road from Inverness to Aberdeen.

---

33 Kevin Bending, *Achieve Your Aim*, Woodfield, 2005, p.25

Another 97 Squadron pilot, WO Stanley Harrison, later wrote up an account of the occasion:

> Squadron songs were bellowed aggressively and replied to by other squadrons; there were competitions to plaster squadron logos on hotel and pub walls and ceilings, and the little town became unrecognisable to its inhabitants. Certainly I never saw scenes to compare with it. Happily, everyone seemed in good humour, there were no fights and damage to property was superficial. The publicans were well repaid by their enormous profit on those three carnival nights.[34]

Finally, on 27 April, the weather cleared and the attack was launched by 43 aircraft from the five squadrons. It was a long flight, with over eight hours in the air, but it was not successful. David reported that he:

> dropped 4000 lb bomb from 8000 feet. Bomb seen to burst and flash lit up the end of the ship – primary being attacked. Burst assumed between ship and cliff. Released 500 lb bombs on island west of target on flak and searchlight, bursts not observed. Trip in and out uneventful.[35]

The Lancaster crews watched as the Halifaxes ran in at low level to lay their mines, dodging the flak and searchlights. But there was no sign of a significant underwater explosion and four Halifaxes and one Lancaster from 97 Squadron, piloted by Flt Lt Mackid, were lost.

They had to do it all again the following day, when a total of 34 aircraft from the same detachment were despatched. The *Tirpitz*, however, remained stubbornly undamaged. The flak was heavier this time, as the German gunners were obviously better prepared.

The next evening, the crews flew back to Woodhall, where they earned a rollicking from the acting CO, Wg Cdr Leonard Slee (later to turn up at RAF Scampton escorting Queen Elizabeth on the day she and the King met the crews who flew on Operation Chastise). Slee had heard reports of the drunken carousing in Elgin, and was not impressed. Painting squadron numbers on pub walls, thereby telling the locals and any German spies among them which squadrons were in town, was a breach of security and drunken behaviour was a breach of discipline.

---

34 Stanley Harrison, *A Bomber Command Survivor*, Sage Pages, 1992, p.97
35 AIR 27/766

David Maltby relaxing, probably at RAF Woodhall Spa, in the early part of 1942. The dog was called Shep, and was adopted as a mascot by his crew.

PHOTO: KEVIN LANCEY

May 1942 saw a slight scaling back in operations across the whole of 5 Group. With more Lancasters becoming available there was a need for crews to be trained in flying them. Some 97 Squadron pilots were sent off on training duties even though they had not yet finished their tours. The rest flew a mixture of mine-laying and bombing operations. On one bombing raid on 4 May David had a very eventful trip. Bound for Stuttgart, he crossed the French coast near Dunkirk and encountered very heavy flak. The aircraft's undercarriage came down of its own accord and so David was forced to turn back. Over the Channel, he tried to open the bomb bays to jettison his load, but the mechanism was also damaged and would not work. He made it back to Woodhall, but had to land with a full load and without flaps. The aircraft – one of the batch seen in production by the King and Queen at the Yeadon factory along with Q-Queenie – was a complete write off, as he overshot the runway and crashed. Fortunately no one in the crew was injured.

He was back in the air three days later, with a mine-laying raid near Kiel and flew on a further five operations later in May, including trips to

Warnemunde and Mannheim. His mine-laying trip to the 'Great Belt' on Tuesday 26 May was his 27th operation.

Crew No. 21 had jelled well as a crew and were obviously good friends outside the aircraft. They even adopted an Alsatian dog called Shep as their mascot. It's not clear who it actually belonged to, but it can be seen both in a picture of David, where he is sitting outside one of the huts on the base reading a newspaper, and in the official squadron aircrew picture – the only dog among a hundred or more airmen! However the crew knew that they would shortly have to split up, as David was getting towards the magic number of 30 operations, usually regarded as the number needed to complete a tour. Also, George Lancey was on the verge of qualifying as a 1st pilot, and the new breed of flight engineers were beginning to arrive at Woodhall.

But first there was a personal matter to be attended to: David and Nina were getting married, an event to which the whole crew was invited. The date had been set for Saturday 30 May, at St Andrew's Church in Wickhambreaux. They had to get married between David's 22nd birthday on 10 May and Nina's 23rd birthday on 31 May so that, as Nina used to joke, their ages would be the same on the marriage certificate. She didn't want to be seen as a cradle-snatcher.

The invitation, typeset in Madonna Ronde font, is on a single heavy card, the size of a postcard. On the back, in Nina's handwriting, are the travel arrangements. A train from Victoria to Canterbury – that dreadful railway journey through Kent that takes an interminable 1hr 50mins to travel 62 miles – and half an hour on a bus would get the visitors to Wickhambreaux in plenty of time. However they wouldn't have very long at the reception if they were going to get back to Lincolnshire that night – the bus back to Canterbury left at 4.50pm.

George Lancey's sister Mollie, who is still alive and well and living in Canada, recalls the occasion well. She was also in England during the war, remembers meeting David and is positive that George and the rest of the crew went to the wedding. Most of them must have left early to get back to Woodhall because plans were underway there for 97 Squadron's participation in a major new type of operation, the Thousand Bomber Raid. Sixteen of the squadron's crews would take part in this raid, with some pilots being recalled from training duties and the squadron commander, Wg Cdr John Collier leading by example, with a scratch crew. However, crew No. 21 did not fly together: Max

Mr. & Mrs. S. G. Goodson
request the company of

" Crew no. 21 "

at the marriage of their daughter

Georgina, with Flying Officer David J. H. Maltby,
*at St. Andrew's Church, Wickhambreaux,
on Saturday, May 30th, 1942, at 1·45 p.m.,*

and afterwards at
Frognall,
Wickhambreaux,

P.T.O.

Train leaves Victoria 10·35
Change Faversham
Arrives Canterbury 12·24
Bus leaves Canterbury 12·50
Arrives Wickhambreaux 1·20

Train leaves Canterbury for
London 5·48 —
Bus leaves Wichambreaux
to catch this train 4·50
arriving at Canterbury 5·25

Buses in case we can't
get Taxis !

Invitation to the wedding of Georgina (Nina) Goodson and David Maltby, 30 May 1942. Nina's handwritten instructions on the back show how it was just about possible to get from Lincolnshire to Kent and back on the day, although a lot of the time would have been spent on trains and buses.

PHOTO: KEVIN LANCEY

David and Nina Maltby after their wedding, flanked by Nina's sister Bettie and her husband Woodroffe Walter.   PHOTO: ALAN THOMPSON

Smith and Harvey Legace were loaned out to other crews, while George Lancey flew as 2nd pilot in an aircraft captained by a Sqn Ldr Stenner. This doesn't even appear in the list of crews from 97 Squadron who flew on the operation. Sqn Ldr Charles Stenner was in 106 Squadron at the time, so we can only assume that this was another scratch crew made up for the occasion.

The Thousand Bomber Raid was Air Marshal Harris's brainchild, designed to show the Chiefs of Staff and the politicians the power that had been built up in Bomber Command. He wanted to mount a 'spectacular' that would 'impress his superiors, attract the admiration of the Americans and Russians who were now Britain's allies, bring cheer to British civilians, and frighten Germany.'[36] He reckoned that, with careful planning, he could get a thousand or more aircraft to drop their bombs on one target in 90 minutes, and that would do the trick. He only had 400 or so front line aircraft – the rest had to come from the operational training units. A huge effort was made to get enough crews and aircraft ready and by 26 May, the day of David's mine-laying trip in the Great Belt area, the force was assembled.

The particular innovation which made such a massive raid possible

36 Patrick Bishop, *Bomber Boys*, Harper Press, 2007, p.97

was the introduction of the 'bomber stream'. All aircraft would fly by the same route out and back, at the same speed, with each one being allotted a height band and a time slot to avoid collisions. The force would then pass through the minimum number of German night-fighter boxes. As each box controller could direct a maximum of just six interceptions per hour, the theory was that they would be overwhelmed by the sheer numbers.

It was decided to bomb Cologne. There was no pretence that they were going for military or industrial targets: the aiming point for the 153 aircraft from 5 Group was the square in front of Cologne Cathedral. Area bombing – Harris's controversial technique which has been frequently criticised since – was to take place on a grand scale.

In bombing terms, the Thousand Bomber Raid was a great success. A total of 1,455 tons of bombs were dropped. More than 12,000 non-domestic buildings and nearly 40,000 dwelling units were destroyed or damaged. The human casualties were also a new record: almost 500 people were killed on the ground in Cologne, of whom only 58 were from the military. Of the 1,047 aircraft eventually despatched, 41 were lost, an 'acceptable' 3.9 per cent of the attacking force.

There was understandable pleasure in the way in which the British press reported the raids: 'Over 1,000 bombers raid Cologne. Biggest Attack of the War. 2,000 tons of bombs in 40 minutes' read the headlines in *The Times*.

However one pilot who might have been expected to take his place in the bomber stream was otherwise engaged in St Andrew's Church, Wickhambreaux. (By coincidence, another pilot who missed the raid was Guy Gibson, then commanding 106 Squadron. He was in hospital, with what was probably an ear infection.) Like most wartime weddings David and Nina's was a low-key affair. The bridegroom was in his best uniform complete with cap rather than his customary forage hat. With no hope of getting a white dress, Nina was in a smart looking outfit with a little hat at a jaunty angle. If they went on a honeymoon, it must have been brief, because by 8 June David was back at RAF Woodhall. Crew No 21 had now been dispersed: George Lancey flew some more operations in June and July as 2nd pilot with two or three other pilots. In August later that year, when he qualified as a 1st pilot, he teamed up again with Max Smith, Pop Humphrey and Harold Rouse, and they flew together for most of the rest of his first tour.

Aircrew of 97 Squadron pose for a photo, summer 1942. David Maltby is third from the left in the second row, seated on a chair. Shep, the dog, is between the two aircrew seated on the ground, fourth and fifth from the right. George Lancey is crouching next to Shep. Max Smith, Harold Rouse and Harvey Legace are thought to be respectively sixth, fourth and second from the right in the front row.

On Monday 8 June David flew on a raid to Essen with a different crew: Plt Offs Briant and Dorward, Sgt Desmond and Flt Sgts Concannon, Jones and Bale. It was a fairly uneventful night although he had a problem with his 4,000 lb 'cookie', which was jettisoned four seconds late. No. 97 Squadron provided six of the 170 aircraft that flew that night. This was David's 28th operation, and the last of his tour. Ettrick wrote in his diary:

> D ops over Essen (28) (total hours ops 161.10) then taken off ops until the great raid on the Dams on May 16th 1943

This is another entry that was obviously written some considerable time after the event, probably after David's death. In fact, David was supposed to fly on at least one other operation: on Thursday 11 June he

was listed to take part in minelaying in the Frisians but his aircraft developed a faulty fuel gauge and could not go. When he went through David's logbook later, Ettrick didn't bother to record this abortive trip, or may not even have noticed it. In his diary entry for 11 June, written at the time, he wrote 'D off ops to Wigsley (till 27 Aug)' and two days later he added a more fervently felt remark: '13 June: David off ops – God be praised'.

Chapter 6

✳

Between Tours

With all the stops and starts he had endured, it had taken David a full year to complete his first tour of operations. Most pilots with a tour under their belts were sent off to training units to help with the training of new recruits, and at first this appears to be what the RAF had in store for David. The 97 Squadron Operations Record Book (ORB) records that he was posted to 1654 Heavy Conversion Unit at RAF Wigsley on 14 June 1942. His rank was still being recorded as Flying Officer. This particular HCU was officially established the following day and facilitated by the amalgamation of two previous 'conversion' flights. Just a month later, on 14 July, he was moved to take charge of a specialist Air Bomber Training Section in No. 1485 Target Towing and Gunnery Flight, as a Flight Lieutenant. Although the flight was formally based at Scampton, it seems that the air bombers were trained at Wigsley for another six weeks. On 27 August they were all to move to Dunholme Lodge, a satellite of Scampton.

During the war years, these kind of flights were formed and disbanded fairly quickly so not a lot of information is available about them. However, I was lucky in this case. There is a meticulously kept Operations Record Book in the National Archives, where the names of officers who served as instructors are recorded.[37] It lists days in which towing facilities or fighter affiliation practice were provided to various squadrons, and the numbers of trainees who arrived for each of the various courses.

Once again the internet came to my aid when I was looking for further information. On a Second World War People's History section of the BBC website I came across a posting from Hugh Aitken, who served in this flight with David, and remembers him well. By contacting the library where his interview was typed I was able to trace him, and he gave me a lot of information about this period of David's service.

No. 1485 Flight had a number of instructors, mainly experienced pilots, bomb aimers and gunners. Groups of trainees would arrive and stay for a few days or sometimes weeks, practising and developing their skills. They used the bombing range at Wainfleet in the Wash for target practice. Gunnery practice took place on ground butts and in the air on drogues towed behind slow flying Lysanders. Hugh remembers that there were at least two Manchesters (by then pretty much retired from front-line squadron duties), as well as Hampdens, Whitleys, Oxfords, Wellingtons and Ansons.

Hugh had started in the RAF as groundcrew, but wanted to train as a wireless operator for aircrew. He went to the famous wireless training school in the Winter Gardens in Blackpool, and passed the initial course there. However, becoming airborne required another medical, and he turned out to be colour blind, which ruled out flying operationally. He realises now that this greatly increased his chances of living to a ripe old age!

He was posted first of all to 1485 Flight when it was at Scampton, and then on to Dunholme and Fulbeck. At one point, keen to get the extra 1s 6d a day 'danger money', he worked as an airborne winch operator, letting out the drogue from a Lysander. When he learnt that one of his predecessors had been accidentally shot while doing this job, he decided that ground-based work was preferable. He still managed to fly on a few occasions, and one Sunday took part in a dummy exercise with the Home Guard, dropping flour bags as simulated bombs. Some of these accidentally fell on a churchyard, showering a congregation dressed in their Sunday best on their way to worship – an incident that caused somewhat fraught relations with local people.

David's relaxed attitude when dealing with other people must have developed here, in his first formal taste of command. Hugh Aitken remembers him as a tall man, a nice commanding officer and very friendly. I have spoken to a number of other people who knew David in the service, and all of them remember him – more than 60 years later – as being friendly and not at all stand-offish. It's often noted that the two most famous COs of 617 Squadron, Guy Gibson and Leonard Cheshire, had contrasting styles of 'man management'. Gibson believed in leading by example: a combination of snobbery and bombast meaning that he didn't tolerate people who didn't share his 'press-on' attitude and almost fanatical hatred of the enemy. Cheshire, however, was an inspirer. Someone who served under him later in the war was greeted on the day they first met with an enthusiasm 'that made you feel he had been waiting to see you all day'.[38] (Anyone who has worked in any large organisation and had a boss who has this attitude will always remember it: I had one once who would drive you demented by keeping you waiting 30 minutes for a scheduled meeting, and then disarm you totally with his 'My dear old friend' approach. You forgave him immediately, and did whatever he wanted.) When he died, David was already at Squadron Leader rank, and was a flight commander in one of the RAF's premier bombing squadrons. If he had survived, he would surely have become a squadron CO within a few months, and who knows what after that.

In October 1943, the Flight moved to Fulbeck, just west of Newark, in the same area where the Maltby family had many connections. It's unlikely that David had much time to look round old haunts, but he was able to get down to Devon with Nina for a short break in November. Ettrick wrote in his diary on 9 November: 'D & Nina came for 3 days. Audrey also here. A unwell. A very tense time.' Why was it tense, I have to wonder? Did they know that Nina was in the early stages of pregnancy? Then, underneath, in a different pen he has recorded poignantly: 'The last time D was here.'

Somewhere around this time, Hugh Aitken remembers being given a lift when David flew down to Cambridge one day, which was convenient for him as he could visit his family. His fiancée was working on codes and ciphers at the famous Bletchley Park, although he didn't find out any details about what she did there until well after the war.

Ettrick doesn't say where David and Nina spent that Christmas, although it's likely it was in Woodhall. Audrey and Jean both came to Witherdon, he notes, and it was 'a dull day'. Audrey's husband Johnnie was away in the army, and she was six months pregnant. Jean went on to Audrey's house in Tunbridge Wells, and was there on New Year's Eve. On 5 January, she went to stay with David and Nina. At the time, she was probably still training as a chef, at college in Gloucester, and the new term had not yet started.

Back on 11 August 1942, David had been awarded the Distinguished

---

38 Sqn Ldr Tony Iveson, quoted in Bishop, *Bomber Boys*, p.192.

Flying Cross (DFC). This was pretty much a standard award for any officer who had completed a tour of operations (NCOs got a Distinguished Flying Medal) but it must still have been a welcome recognition of a momentous and dangerous year. So on 8 February the whole family went up to London to attend his investiture ceremony. Eight of them stayed at the Piccadilly Hotel, and went to see the Cicely Courtneidge show at the Palace Theatre one night and the play 'A Quiet Weekend' at the Lansdowne the next.

Chapter 7

No 617 Squadron

On Wednesday 17 March 1943 David reported back to 97 Squadron at the familiar RAF Woodhall Spa to start his second tour. The next day, bomb aimer John Fort, flight engineer William Hatton, navigator Vivian Nicholson, wireless operator Antony Stone, bomb aimer John Fort, air gunners Harold Simmonds and Austin Williams, and flight engineer William Hatton all arrived, after just a month in 207 Squadron at RAF Langar. This was a complete crew except, of course, a pilot. These six men had all come together in a Lancaster conversion unit at RAF Swinderby at the beginning of the year, but they arrived there by a variety of routes.

Vivian Nicholson
By common consent the navigator was the next most skilled person in a heavy bomber crew after the pilot. In David Maltby's team that role was performed by its youngest member, a smiling lad with crinkly hair from Co Durham, Vivian Nicholson. The Nicholson family came from Sherburn, once one of the dozens of pit communities that ring the city of Durham, and now a commuter village. Before nationalisation, the local mines were owned by the Lambton family, and the pub at the village crossroads still bears their name. (The sometime head of the family, Viscount Lambton, had his moment in the national limelight when he had to resign from the Heath government in the 1970s after his affair with a prostitute was exposed. The press photos of the time show him in a pair of particularly sinister dark glasses, which added to his somewhat seedy reputation.) The collieries closed in the 1950s, but at the time the Nicholson family were growing up many local people were employed there.

Vivian was the eldest of eight children, all boys. I sat in his brother

is a photo of Mick Smith, a lad Sheffield and myself, in our work coveralls. We have been pals, with Harry Sherwood, (and Doc. Webb from Willington if he had been with us. poor lad). right through our course from London to Tuscaloosa. He is [...] as well as myself.

Vivian

Best from U.S.A.
A merry Xmas.

Vivian Nicholson photographed with his friend Mick Smith while training in the USA, probably in December 1941. Even before the USA entered the war many RAF personnel were sent there for aircrew training. Note the white flash on their caps, indicating they were trainees. PHOTO: NICHOLSON FAMILY

Cyril's house on a summer morning as he went through the names: Vivian, Arthur, Cyril, Everett, Ian, Ivan, Raymond and Francis. Two died young: Ian at the age of 8, and Ivan in infancy. Two more now live in the USA. Cyril, Raymond and Francis still live locally, Cyril in the same street in which he was brought up, in a house his parents also once owned. Vivian's parents – Arthur and Elizabeth – and their boys were a respectable church-going family and their paternal grandfather, Harle Nicholson, was the local churchwarden. The family album still shows a photo with three of the boys in identical smart Sunday suits. Arthur Nicholson had a joinery and undertaking business, and also owned some of the houses in the village. When he left the local school, Vivian was apprenticed in the family business but then, even before he turned 18, he volunteered to join the RAF.

After initial training in No.1 Initial Training Wing in Babbacombe, near Torquay, he was packed off to Canada on the British Commonwealth Air Training Plan. Canada, with its wide open spaces and distance from the main theatres of conflict in Europe, was ideal for aircrew training, and over 150,000 people from Britain, the Commonwealth countries and the USA, were sent there during the war. He started his training in Canada but then went on to Tuscaloosa, Alabama in the USA for part of his course. Even though the USA was not yet in the war, it was already providing training facilities for the Allies.

In December 1941, round about the time the Japanese attacked Pearl Harbor and brought the USA into the war, he sent his parents a picture of himself and 'a lad from Sheffield' called Mick Smith. 'We have been pals, with Harry Sherwood, (and Doc Webb from Willington if he had been with us, poor lad) right through our course from London to Tuscaloosa.' He added: 'All the best from U.S.A. A merry Xmas.'

Besides the training in navigation itself, there were a number of other courses the aspiring navigators needed to pass, such as map reading, armaments, Morse Code, instrument and radio direction-finding, reconnaissance and aerial photography. Navigation itself required a lot of mathematical skill. No calculators or other mechanical help existed then, although there were complicated slide rules which helped with some of the calculations. A navigator had to learn how to find the position of his aircraft using 'dead reckoning'. By knowing the direction, speed and course on which you were travelling you were able to work out your 'air position'. This you compared with your 'ground position' by recording the time you reached various known places on your map. You could therefore calculate the variation caused by the wind – the 'drift' – and tell the pilot which course to set. That was the theory, at least, but of course in practice it was much more difficult.[39]

---

39 Taylor and Davidson, *Bomber Crew*, pp.235-241

By the late summer of 1942 Vivian's specialist navigator training was at an end, and the work of getting him ready to fly in a bomber crew began. He was sent to No.10 OTU at RAF St Eval, Cornwall, in September 1942. He arrived there at the same time as bomb aimer John Fort and wireless operator Antony Stone, and it is likely that the trio teamed up there. Some of the training flights in this Unit took place on anti-submarine patrols in Whitley aircraft, but it doesn't seem that Vivian took part in these. All three arrived at No.1660 Conversion Unit at RAF Swinderby in January 1943, at the same time as William Hatton and Harold Simmonds, and probably crewed up there. A month or so later, they were ready for operations and they all left for 207 Squadron at RAF Langar in Nottinghamshire.

Antony Stone

Winchester's sometime town crier, Alan Kinge, has done a lot to keep the story of Antony Stone and his family in the forefront of local people's minds by writing articles in the local press and organising an exhibition in the city library. I was lucky enough to track down Alan with the help of the library, and he passed on to me what he knew about the family history, and contact details for the family.

Antony Joseph Bazeley Stone was the younger son of a family of two boys. His older brother Edgar is still alive but was not well enough to talk to me when I contacted the family early in 2007. Edgar's son Michael, however, was happy to help. Born a few years after the war, like me, Michael remembers hearing a lot about his uncle when he was growing up, but of course, never met him.

Edgar and Antony's father, Joseph Stone, had an eventful life. He was Jewish, and had been born in Russia at the end of the 19th century. The family legend is that he was brought to London by the Rothschild family, who were certainly involved in helping Jewish families escape the pogroms of the time. He trained as a barber in Hackney and joined the Rifle Brigade at the beginning of the First World War. This brought him to Winchester, and he stayed there after the war where he met and married a Hampshire girl called Dorothy Grace Bazeley. Joe set up as a barber in a shop in Jewry Street in the city. Their second son was born at home in Nuns Road, Winchester on 5 December 1920.

Antony went first to the local Hyde School and sang in the choir at St Bartholomew's Church. A picture of the choir still exists and a

Hyde School, near Winchester, in about 1926. Antony Stone is second from the left in the front row.   PHOTO: ALAN KINGE

school friend, Alan House, recalls that no fewer than four other boys besides Antony were later to join the RAF. Antony then went to Peter Symonds School in Winchester. He decided to train as a chef, and went up to London to do so, studying at the Westminster Technical Institute. He worked at various well known restaurants, including Quaglino's, the Dorchester and the Ritz, cooking at one time, Michael recalls being told, for the King and Queen.

In 1940 he volunteered for the RAF, and was called up in November 1940 to the same Reception Centre at Uxbridge as David had been through a few months earlier. He was selected for wireless operator training, and passed through various training centres at Thorney Island, Yatesbury and Bassingbourn.

Training as a wireless operator not only involved the obvious: sending and receiving of signals and learning Morse Code but by the end of the course operators had to be able to read and transmit Morse Code at a speed of at least 18 words a minute. There were also a large number of 'Q codes' which had to be memorised. These were three letter codes all beginning with 'Q' that were requests or instructions to be sent to and from the base, covering such things as requests from the base for

Top: Jewry Street, Winchester in the 1930s. Joseph Stone's hairdressers can be seen to the left of Millett's, which is on the corner.

Right: Antony Stone in about 1942, soon after qualifying as a Wireless Operator / Air Gunner.

weather updates (QBZ) or from the aircraft for permission to land (QFO). Wireless training also meant gaining a lot of theoretical and practical knowledge about radios and all the other electrical equipment on board. This meant that the wireless operator on a heavy bomber often picked up other ancillary duties. On Operation Chastise, for instance, it became his job to start and supervise the rotation mechanism for the special mine ten minutes before the bombing run began.

At the time Antony was passing through the system, wireless operators also had to have gunnery training, although this requirement was removed later in the war. His last piece of specialist training was therefore at No.1 Air Gunnery School, at RAF Pembrey in Carmarthenshire. Then it was on to No.10 OTU at St Eval, where his path crossed with Vivian Nicholson and John Fort.

By the time he arrived at 617 Squadron Antony was engaged to a nurse at the Royal Hampshire County Hospital, Peggy Henstridge, although it's not certain when the relationship began.

John Fort

John Fort was born on the Lancashire side of the Pennines, in the cotton town of Colne, on 14 January 1912. He was one of six brothers. After attending Christchurch School in the town, he went into the RAF in 1929 to train as an apprentice, going to the No. 1 School of Technical Training at RAF Halton in Buckinghamshire. This was the famous training establishment set up by Lord Trenchard ('the father of the RAF') to supply the technicians needed to support aircrew and maintain aircraft. After completing the three year course he was posted to the Central Flying School and then went to sea in the aircraft carrier HMS Glorious.(Between 1918 and 1937 the RAF operated the aircraft which flew on aircraft carriers, and supplied its own ground staff to service them.)

Back on dry land, he continued in groundcrew until the second year of the war, when he volunteered for aircrew training. Selected as a specialist bomb aimer (or air bomber, to give the job its proper name) he went off to a Bombing and Gunnery School, where students were taught a lot of theory as well as the practical aspects, such as map reading and simulator training, learning exactly where to drop the weapon. They moved on to practice air-to-ground bombing runs over ranges where they dropped 25 lb smoke bombs.

John Fort, in his 617 Squadron days.
PHOTO: PETER FORT / ALEX BATEMAN

This is where they developed the real skills. The bomb aimer took over the navigation of the aircraft from the navigator as they approached the target and began a bombing run. It was he who would call out to the pilot over the intercom the small direction changes needed, from his position lying flat out in the nose. From a height of 1,000 ft, the bomb aimer would be expected to be able to hit a target with an accuracy of under 50 yards.[40]

At the end of his course John had done well enough to be offered a commission and so it was as a Pilot Officer he arrived at No.10 OTU in September 1942, at RAF St Eval. After completing the course there, where he also met Vivian Nicholson and Antony Stone, he went with them to 1660 Conversion Unit, and on to 207 Squadron. The citation for the DFC that he later received for Operation Chastise says that he had completed one operation before joining 617 Squadron. As there appears to be no record of him flying on an operation in 207 Squadron, he may have been credited with one while at the OTU, as some anti-submarine patrols were flown from there.

---

40 Taylor and Davidson, *Bomber Crew,* pp.101-103

Harold Simmonds, photographed in Warrington, Cheshire, in 1942 with his girlfriend, Phyllis.   PHOTO: GRACE BLACKBURN

Harold Simmonds

Harold Thomas Simmonds was born on Christmas Day 1921, the only son of Thomas and Elizabeth Simmonds. Their only daughter, Grace, was some five years younger. His parents were both from Burgess Hill in East Sussex, and they settled in the town after they had married. They had met while they were both working in service, Thomas as a gardener.

Burgess Hill has expanded hugely since the 1920s, and is now firmly within the London commuter area, but when Harold and Grace were growing up, it only had a population of a few thousand. However, 90 men from the town and the surrounding area were killed during the Second World War, and are commemorated in the publication *The Men of Burgess Hill,* compiled by Guy Voice. Would that every town in Britain had a similar publication – research like mine would have been made a lot easier!

41   Taylor and Davidson, Bomber Crew, pp.106–108

Harold went to London Road School and later worked in a government job. Soon after the war started, Harold volunteered for the RAF. He started his service in groundcrew, serving at Kemble in Gloucestershire and Mount Batten near Plymouth. However, he had always wanted to fly, and eventually he was selected for aircrew training, going to the No.2 Air Gunners School in Dalcross, near Inverness.

At some point in 1942 he started going out with a girl called Phyllis, although his sister Grace doesn't recall her surname, or where they met. She does have a photograph of the pair together, which was captioned as being taken in Warrington, Cheshire, in 1942.

The training for gunnery took less time than for any of the specialist jobs in a Lancaster, but the trainees still had to spend up to 13 weeks firing guns on the ground and later at drogues towed by aircraft. They also had to learn how to fix faults, strip their guns down and maintain them – essential skills if they were to keep them working while up in the air. Sometimes they were blindfolded when practicing these skills, just to make the conditions more difficult.[41]

The training system meant that gunners and flight engineers only joined up with navigators, bomb aimers and wireless operators on the final stage of the process, in the Conversion Unit. Thus it was that Harold Simmonds first met Vivian Nicholson, John Fort and Antony Stone at 1660 Conversion Unit at Swinderby, when they were all posted there on 5 January 1943.

William Hatton

The last of the five who crewed up with David Maltby at 97 Squadron, and were to fly on the Dams Raid two months later, was flight engineer William Hatton. Born in Wakefield on 24 March 1920, he was one of four children: two boys and two girls. He went to Holy Trinity and Thornes House School in the town.

Like Harold Simmonds, with whom he later became friendly enough to give him a photo which was found in Harold's personal effects, when Bill first joined the RAF he was placed in groundcrew, training at both No.10. and No.2 Schools of Technical Training. In May 1941, he went to RAF Speke in Liverpool and worked servicing aircraft in the Merchant Ship Fighter Unit. This was a short lived scheme whereby Hawker Hurricanes were sent to sea on special merchant ships, which were equipped with catapults for launching them. The

William Hatton.
Photograph probably
taken in late 1942, as
he is wearing his Flight
Engineer's brevet.

PHOTO: GUY VOICE

plan was to enable the Hurricanes to be launched far out at sea to help protect the Atlantic convoys. The only drawback was that they had no way of landing, so the pilot had to bale out of the Hurricane and let the aircraft fall into the sea. As his spell there drew to a close, the opportunity arose for experienced groundcrew to become flight engineers on heavy bombers. Bill applied and was sent to the only flight engineer training facility, No.4 School of Technical Training at RAF St Athan.

The job of the flight engineer was to look after some of the controls (such as fuel consumption) that previously had been the responsibility of a qualified pilot. They were also expected to cope with any mechanical problems which arose while airborne. Most flight engineers were also given some rudimentary flying training, so that they could keep the aircraft on a level course if the pilot needed a short break, or in an emergency.[42] After qualifying as a flight engineer, Bill went on to Swinderby, to join 1660 Conversion Unit, where he was to join up with the four others listed above.

The final member of the crew was Victor Hill, the front gunner, but as he didn't join the Maltby crew until Friday 7 May his story will be left until later. (See p.99.)

We know that Nicholson, Stone, Fort, Simmonds, Hatton and Williams all joined 207 Squadron on 17 February 1943 and stayed there for less than a month. Three pilots also joined 207 Squadron from 1660 Conversion Unit on the same day, but none of them seem to have been attached to this crew. The 207 Squadron records are confusing, and it is therefore not clear what they did in this time. They would probably have been treated as 'spares' for a while, which is why William Hatton flew on two operations on 26 and 27 February, with two different pilots. There are entries in the 207 Squadron Operations Record Book during March for a Sgt V Nicholson, a Sgt I H Nicholson, a Sgt J Simmons and a Sgt H T Simmonds, sometimes flying with the same pilot, sometimes with different ones.[43] However, entries for both versions of these names are still appearing at the end of March 1943, by which time we know that both Vivian Nicholson and Harold Simmonds were training at 617 Squadron, so there is obviously some sort of error in the records.

What is clear is that the 207 Squadron ORB states that they were all posted out to 97 Squadron on 15 March. It seems likely that because there was no spare pilot for them to work with as a crew, it was therefore decided to send them on to another squadron which had a pilot available. They are recorded in the 97 Squadron ORB as arriving at Woodhall Spa on 18 March.

They were teamed up with David, and spent several days in routine training flights, and getting used to each other. Ten days after they all arrived at Woodhall, they were moved together as a crew to the new squadron at Scampton.

✳   ✳   ✳

---

42 Taylor and Davidson, *Bomber Crew*, p.113
43   AIR 27/1234

While David and his new crew were getting acquainted at Woodhall Spa, a few miles away, at 5 Group headquarters in Grantham, an audacious plan was being developed. After years of experiments and tests, and months of meetings and lobbying, the assistant chief designer of Vickers-Armstrong Aviation Section, Barnes Wallis, had finally been given permission to go ahead with developing a new weapon to attack the German dams in the Ruhr and Eder valleys. Wallis began his final drawings for the weapon, codenamed Upkeep, on Saturday 27 February. The way in which this weapon would be delivered was the subject of much debate in the higher echelons of Bomber Command and, in the second week in March, Air Chief Marshal Harris decided that it should be given to a new squadron rather than taking an existing squadron out of his current 'main force'. He nominated Wg Cdr Guy Gibson as the new squadron's CO, as Gibson had impressed him when Harris had been AOC of 5 Group earlier in the war. Gibson, one of the most experienced and highly decorated bomber pilots in the RAF, had just completed his tour as Commanding Officer of 106 Squadron.

The exact timings of what happened next have been the subject of confusion over the years (not least because Gibson himself muddied the water with his account in *Enemy Coast Ahead,* where he elided some events and invented others). Even the two most authoritative accounts, by John Sweetman and Richard Morris, still disagree on some dates, for instance that of the first meeting between Gibson and Cochrane. It may be helpful, therefore, to set out a chronology from Friday 12 March to Wednesday 31 March as David would have seen it, in a narrative that I have put together with the help of Robert Owen, 617 Squadron's official historian.

Friday 12 March

Gibson finished his tour of operations after a flight to Stuttgart, and prepared to leave RAF Coningsby. His own account says that his new job was supposed to be at Group HQ writing a manual for new bomber pilots, but the adjutant at 106 Squadron, probably writing with hindsight, recorded on Sunday 14 March that Gibson had been posted to 'form a new squadron'.

Wednesday 17 March

At the headquarters of Bomber Command in High Wycombe, the

Senior Air Staff Officer, Air Vice Marshal R D Oxland, wrote two important memos, which officially started the process of forming a new squadron. First he wrote to the G/C Ops at Bomber Command, Air Cdre S O Bufton, stating that the Commander in Chief [Harris] had decided 'this afternoon' that a new squadron should be formed. On the same day his information was passed to the Air Officer Commanding No.5 Group, Air Vice Marshal the Hon Sir Ralph Cochrane. Oxland also wrote directly to Cochrane describing the new weapon called Upkeep, a spherical bomb which if spun and dropped from a height of 100 ft at about 200 mph would travel 1,200 yards.

> It is proposed to use this weapon in the first instance against a large dam in Germany, which, if breached, will have serious consequences in the neighbouring industrial area... The operation against this dam will not, it is thought, prove particularly dangerous, but it will undoubtedly require skilled crews. Volunteer crews will, therefore, have to be carefully selected from the squadrons in your Group.[44]

It is worth noting that the weapon is here called a spherical bomb, but after further trials the design was changed to a large cylinder, much the shape and size of the roller used on a cricket field. This was also the day on which the 97 Squadron Operations Record book records the return to the Squadron of 'F/L G. H. Maltby [sic] from 1485 S & G Flight [sic]'.

Thursday 18 March
In the afternoon, Gibson was called in to meet Cochrane, and asked to do 'one last trip.' (Morris says that this meeting happened on Monday 15 March.) In Enemy Coast Ahead, Gibson wrote that nothing happened for two days after that, but in fact it seems that there was a gap of only one day. The 97 Squadron ORB records the transfer of Fort, Hatton, Nicholson, Stone, Simmonds and Williams from 207 Squadron on this day.

Friday 19 March
Gibson was called to another meeting with Cochrane. This time the Station Commander of RAF Scampton, Air Cdre Charles Whitworth, was also present. Gibson was asked to form a special squadron. Gibson says that he then spent another two days at Grantham in meetings

---

44 AIR 14/840, quoted in Sweetman, *Dambusters Raid*, p.97

selecting 'equipment, bodies, erks [groundcrew], aircrew'. Two of the people he names: the man with the red moustache called Cartwright, and a Sqn Ldr May – the others obviously made less of an impression on him. He says that it took him an hour to pick his pilots, and that he wrote the names down on a piece of paper and handed them over.

> I had picked them all myself because from my own personal knowledge I believed them to be the best bomber pilots available. I knew that each one of them had already done his full tour of duty and should really now be having a well-earned rest; and I knew also that there was nothing any of them would want less than this rest when they heard that there was an exciting operation on hand.[45]

It is this paragraph that has led to the myth that the pilots at 617 Squadron were personally selected by Gibson. He goes on to compound the story with a description of finding them all waiting for him, and an impromptu party in the officers' mess, on the day he arrived at Scampton. Paul Brickhill repeats this version of events in *The Dam Busters* book, and the movie follows the same course, with both giving a supporting role to Gibson's pint-drinking dog, the famous Nigger.

The truth is that the process was much more drawn out, and the crews arrived over a period of about 10 days. It is probable that the only pilots destined for the new squadron who could have been at Scampton on the day Gibson arrived were those who were to be transferred from 57 Squadron, which was also based there. He could not possibly have spent the first evening knocking back pints with most of them. We know that Gibson certainly asked for some pilots by name, because he spoke to Mick Martin, Joe McCarthy and David Shannon, and maybe some others, by phone. Why did he choose to over-elaborate the story? The answer, as Richard Morris has discovered, is because Gibson's name appeared on an article, written by a ghost writer, in the *Sunday Express* later in 1943, where the writer – presumably an Air Ministry public relations officer – credited Gibson with the selection not only of all the pilots but of the entire squadron. Choosing twenty or so pilots might just have been feasible, but finding another 120 aircrew was most unlikely. In fact, Gibson didn't even know all of his own crew before they arrived at 617 Squadron, and treated some of its members with an arrogance bordering on contempt. However when the *Sunday*

---

45 Gibson, *Enemy Coast Ahead*, pp.239-240

Officers Mess at RAF Scampton. The doors and ivy look much as they did in 1943, but the pitched roof was added in the 1970s.   PHOTO: CHARLES FOSTER

Express article was incorporated wholesale into the draft of *Enemy Coast Ahead*, Gibson never bothered to change it.[46]

Sunday 21 March

Although Gibson says that he had spent two days at Grantham on administrative duties, once again it must have been not much more than one, since he definitely arrived at Scampton on the Sunday afternoon. No pilots or other aircrew were waiting for him, but it seems that some of the administrative staff must have been ready to start work the next morning. Two NCOs, Flt Sgt G E Powell and Sgt Jim Heveron came from 57 Squadron and were obviously deemed suitable. The Adjutant, however, wasn't and Gibson got rid of him, asking for an old colleague from 106 Squadron, Flt Lt Harry Humphries.

Scampton's yellowy-red brick buildings still look much as they did during the war, except that most of the old flat roofs have been replaced. There is only one flying unit based at the station now – the

46 Morris, *Guy Gibson*, p.148

famous Red Arrows display team – which means that many buildings are unused, but they retain the feel of a pre-war life style. Peering through the windows of the Officers' Mess you can imagine the leather armchairs, the wind-up gramophone, the waiter with the tray of drinks. Here is the rugby pitch, over there the squash courts, there the base of the old cricket pavilion. The four C type hangars form an arc on the south-east side of the airfield, and attached to each is a small two storey administration block. The block attached to No.2 Hangar is the one which housed the 617 Squadron offices, with the squadron commander occupying the top right corner, and the adjutant next to him. One day in July 1943, two months after Operation Chastise, Gibson and David sat in that office, trying to look busy while an Air Ministry photographer shot a series of expensive colour transparencies for publicity purposes.

At the time of Chastise, Scampton still had grass runways. The airfield sits atop a slight escarpment with excellent natural drainage, so the runway area did not often get boggy enough to jeopardise the flying of heavy aircraft. From aerial pictures taken at the time (which can be seen in the small museum in Hangar No. 1) you can see the hedgerows which were painted on the grass to fool any passing German bomber.

Wednesday 24 March

Humphries arrived at Scampton. The new squadron (still unnumbered) was described as being 'formed on ordinary Lancasters'. Some aircrew were ordered to report on this day, but it's not clear whether any actually did. Anyway, Gibson was not there to greet them. He had travelled by train and car down to Weybridge in Surrey for his first meeting with Barnes Wallis. To Wallis's embarrassment, he soon realised that he did not have the authority to divulge the target to Gibson.

Thursday 25 March

The squadron now had a number, 617, and was reported 'ready to fly'. Nine pilots are listed as being transferred to the new Squadron on that day, including the three who came from 97 Squadron: Flt Lts Les Munro, a New Zealander, Joe McCarthy, an American serving in the RCAF, and David Maltby. Their transfer and that of their crews, are all listed in the 97 Squadron Operations Record Book on that day. (The other six pilots transferred on 25 March would seem to have been Flt Lt David Shannon, from 8 Group, Sqn Ldr Henry Maudslay and Plt Off Les Knight from 50 Squadron, Flg Off Norman Barlow from 61 Squadron and Sgts Cyril Anderson and Bill Townsend from 49 Squadron.)

Les Munro and Joe McCarthy were both coming towards the end of their first tours. David was starting his second. In recent correspondence with me Les wrote:

> I distinctly remember discussing with my crew the question of whether we should volunteer or not, and I seem to think that Joe McCarthy did likewise on the same day. I was not aware of how or when David reached his decision. Can't remember how I was advised that our transfer to Scampton was official, but it was certainly not by Gibson.

He is also fairly sure that they all transferred the few miles to Scampton in a crew bus, and has the distinct memory of a gathering in the ante-room of the Officers' Mess in the evening.[47] Perhaps this was the evening that Gibson wrote about in *Enemy Coast Ahead*, although some of the pilots, such as Mick Martin, were still not at Scampton by this Thursday. (Martin arrived on Wednesday 31 March.)

Saturday 27 March

Gibson at least began to get a better idea of what was expected from the squadron when a set of 'most secret' orders was given to him by Gp Capt H V Satterly, Senior Air Staff Officer at 5 Group. Without being told the exact targets, Gibson was informed that the squadron would be attacking a number of lightly defended targets in moonlight with a final approach at 100 ft at a precise speed of about 240mph. The orders stated that, in preparation for the attack, it would be 'convenient to practise this over water' and crews should be able to release their 'mine' within 40 yards of a specified release point. Night flying would be simulated by making the pilot and bomb aimer wear special amber coloured goggles with blue Perspex screens fitted to the windows.

By now, a number of ordinary Lancasters had arrived for training purposes and in the afternoon, the first crew got airborne. Flt Lt Bill Astell was despatched to photograph nine lakes that Satterly had identified as being suitable for practice.

---

47 Les Munro, email to author, 8 May 2007

Sunday 28 March

Gibson decided to try out low flying over water himself. With Hopgood and Young on board, he went off to Derwent Reservoir in Derbyshire. In daylight the flying was not too difficult, but when dusk fell it became a lot harder, and they narrowly avoided an accident.

Monday 29 March

Gibson was summoned to Group HQ and told the target by Cochrane. He was shown models of the Möhne and Sorpe dams – the model of the Möhne, dramatically unveiled to all the crews at the briefing on the day of the raid, can still be seen in the Imperial War Museum.

Wednesday 31 March

Training was gathering pace by this stage, and David and his crew made their first training flight on this day. The Avro factories were still adapting the special Lancasters that 617 Squadron would need for the raid, so for much of April these flights took place on ordinary aircraft. David flew for two hours on what was described as a 'low level cross-country and bombing' exercise.

During the next six weeks, David and his crew would fly on another 23 training flights, mainly low-level cross country and bombing. Various routes had been devised and the reservoirs at Derwent Reservoir in Derbyshire, Eyebrook near Uppingham and Abberton near Colchester were used for runs at low level over water. The Dam Busters film has a scene where a farmer writes a letter of complaint to the Air Ministry about the effect on his egg production. This was based on the truth, as a number of complaints from farmers were received during this period. It's not surprising, the noise generated by flying at the astonishing low level at which they were practising must have been devastating – many church spires are well over 200 ft in height, and the tower of Lincoln Cathedral is 271 ft.

The impression is sometimes given that the crews spent all their time in these six weeks practising, but in fact in that time David and his crew were only airborne on average every other day for a total of some 29 hours. Only three aircraft were equipped with the special tinted cockpit windows which allowed the simulation of night flying, so crews had to take turns, and use other aircraft for other types of training.

There were several gaps of two or three days, and one of five days, between flights.

Meanwhile frantic work was going on at Avro and at Scampton itself adapting the Lancasters, and at various Vickers Armstrong plants by Barnes Wallis and his team developing the 'Upkeep' weapon. The weapon was still being modified as test drops proceeded and in fact a live Upkeep was only dropped for the first time three days before the operation. By 13 May 56 weapons had been delivered to Scampton (many more than the twenty or so which would be needed for this operation – an indication that the Air Ministry was thinking ahead, with the possibility of using it again sometime in the future).

The adapted aircraft, which had the rather odd and cumbersome name of Type 464 Provisioning Lancasters, only arrived in ones and twos. David first flew one on Monday 3 May, taking it for a one hour air test, followed by a bomb dropping practice. It was an odd looking machine, and must have been the object of some attention amongst curious air and groundcrew. The normal Lancaster had been modified by removing the mid-upper gun turret and bomb-bay doors. A special mechanism of a drive belt and callipers were fitted to hold, spin and drop the weapon, powered by the motor normally used to rotate the mid-upper turret. Without this turret, the second gunner would stay permanently in the front gunner position. (On most normal operations, the front guns were operated part-time as necessary, usually by the wireless operator.) The aircraft that David first flew on 3 May was the one he would use on Chastise, Lancaster No. ED906. The code letters AJ-J, which he had been using for most of his training on a normal Lancaster, was transferred over to this one.

It was not uncommon for Second World War RAF pilots to use their own versions for their aircraft letters, rather than the standard Alpha, Bravo, Charlie that we are used to today. Mick Martin, for instance, called his 617 Squadron aircraft P-Popsie. (This lack of standardisation leads to the kind of minor detail that some writers about the Dams Raid often get wrong. David's Lancaster is listed in some books as J-Jig, and in another the author asserts that it was called J-Johnny after the name of his son. In fact J-Johnny was the official phonetic alphabet term in 1943, and J-Jig was a recognised alternative. David's son is certainly called John, but as he was born after Operation Chastise took place, the aircraft could not have been named after him.)

Upkeep 'mine' underneath Gibson's aircraft, AJ-G. The retaining callipers and the chain drive used to rotate it can be clearly seen.   PHOTO: IWM/HU69915

Like all engineering projects a certain amount of 'bodgery' was required to get everything working satisfactorily. Sweetman tells us about the way the groundcrew had to balance each weapon individually. When the mines arrived from the filling factory, they were hung for centrifugal balancing underneath one of the modified Lancasters between two discs, each one of which was itself held by a pair of retaining callipers. The whole apparatus hung down below the aircraft, looking not unlike a pair of cymbals. To balance the mine, a piece of metal plate was bolted to its lighter side, and it was then spun. If the mine was not balanced, then the plate had to be removed, taken back to the machine shop, machined down to remove weight, and then reattached. This process often had to be repeated several times until it worked correctly. In addition, a 'few one thousandth parts of an inch' had to be machined off the brass cup which formed part of the fuse gear.[48]

This all sounds a bit 'Heath Robinsonish', another item to add to the Dambusters legend which already has Barnes Wallis in an overcoat

---

48 Sweetman, *Dambusters Raid*, p.113

with his trouser legs rolled up, using his toes to fish in the sea for bits of test bombs which had broken up. But in fact the process of 'fit and make fit' is perfectly standard, as anybody who has ever built anything mechanical can tell you.

Not much more than a week before the raid was due to take place (although David would not have yet been aware of exactly when this was likely to be) a decision was taken to replace Sgt Austin Williams as front gunner. There appears to have been some sort of disciplinary reason for this, as Williams was then posted to the Air Crew Refresher Course in Brighton. With no other gunners available at Scampton, the net was cast further. No 9 Squadron had just moved from RAF Waddington to RAF Bardney to enable concrete runways to be built at Waddington and amongst its personnel was a spare gunner, Sgt Victor Hill. He was hastily moved the 15 or so miles to Scampton, where he is recorded as arriving on Friday 7 May. When he came back to Scampton at the end of May, Austin Williams was assigned to the crew of Plt Off Bill Divall, who hadn't flown on the raid because of crew sickness. (Divall's was one of the two crews which pulled out at the last minute, a decision which made the final selection easier as there were only nineteen serviceable aircraft, and nineteen crews able to fly.) He stayed with Divall in 617 Squadron for the next four months, and died just 24 hours after his erstwhile crewmates when Divall was shot down over the Dortmund Ems canal on 16 September 1943.

Victor Hill

Unlike the rest of David Maltby's crew, Victor Hill had plenty of operational experience. He had flown 22 operations on Lancasters between October 1942 and March 1943, and had taken part in some of the war's most famous raids, including the daylight raid on the Schneider works at Le Creusot in France.

Victor Hill had been born in Gloucestershire in 1921. He was an only child, the son of Harry and Catherine Hill, who both worked at Berkeley Castle. He was brought up on the castle estate and went to the local school. After leaving school, he also worked at the castle, as a gardener, where he met a girl called Evelyn Hourihane, whom he married in 1941 at about the time he joined the RAF. Evelyn came from the Rhondda in South Wales, and she moved back to Wales to be near her

Victor Hill and Evelyn
Hourihane on their
wedding day in 1941.
PHOTO: VALERIE ASHTON

parents while Vic was away in the RAF, soon after their daughter
Valerie was born.

Vic had been in groundcrew when he first joined up, but volunteered for aircrew and trained as a gunner when the heavy bombers
began to arrive and there were many more chances to fly. His first posting was to 9 Squadron in August 1942, round about the time it was
posted to Waddington and converted to Lancasters from Wellingtons.
He joined a crew piloted by Sgt C McDonald, and flew most of his operations with them. It appears that he was replaced by another gunner
and the crew split up in mid February 1943. Most of the personnel
moved on to 83 Squadron, but Vic was left behind as a spare gunner
and flew on his last operation in 9 Squadron on 8 March, with Sgt
Doolan as the pilot. With 22 operations under his belt, Vic must have
been thinking that he would finish a complete tour in the next two or

Some of the test drops of Upkeep at Reculver, Kent were filmed, and this is a still from one sequence. The bareheaded figure on the left is Barnes Wallis.

PHOTO: IWM/FLM2343

three months. As he made his way to Scampton in early May, he surely didn't realise how significant his next operation would be.

Victor Hill's first flight as a member of David's crew was on Friday 7 May. This is described as a 'bombing run over Wash' in the flight authorisation records, a practice run at night with the new spotlights. Other flights took the crew to Reculver in Kent, where they practised dropping dummy Upkeeps, watching them bounce and roll to a stop up the beach. These practice runs went on for several days, watched by Barnes Wallis. One session was filmed and is in the Imperial War Museum archives – in it the figure of Wallis can be seen, wearing a long overcoat and waving his arms excitedly as his invention demonstrably works.

Long after the war, Valerie Ashton, Vic Hill's daughter, was told by another 617 Squadron gunner Doug Webb, from Bill Townsend's crew, that it was her father who had made the famous suggestion that the front gunner's position should be fitted with stirrups to keep his feet out of the way of the bomb aimer. It made sense to Valerie, as she knew her father had been around horses a lot when working as a gardener.

This rare photograph shows David's Dams Raid Lancaster flying over his wife Nina's family house, Frognall, just outside Wickhambreaux in Kent. It was taken by Nina herself, probably on Wednesday 12 May 1943, when David was practising bombing runs at Reculver. He frequently told Nina when he thought he would be able to fly over, and would waggle the wings of his aircraft to show that it was him. PHOTO: SPITFIRE MEMORIAL MUSEUM, MANSTON

When I asked the only surviving front gunner from the raid, Fred Sutherland, about this theory he said that it might be so, but he had always thought that it must have been a bomb aimer who came up with the idea as they were the ones who were always complaining. The truth is hard to pin down, and has become another part of the Dambuster myth which will probably run and run.

In the week before Chastise, the crew carried out three further low-level training flights, two on Tuesday 11 May and one on Wednesday 12 May. On some of the training flights other passengers were allowed. On one, Gp Capt Whitworth flew with Gibson and WAAF Section Officer Fay Gillon with Mick Martin. Fay Gillon wrote a memorable contemporary account of this trip, which was reproduced by Richard Morris.[49] On the Thursday at 1300 David flew AJ-J to the Avro fitters at

49 Morris, *Guy Gibson*, pp.160-162

Woodford in Cheshire for repair work on the bomb-bay fairing. The Lancaster wasn't ready for him to fly back to Scampton until 2030 the next day, Friday 14 May, and he landed back at Scampton 40 minutes later.

Sweetman tells us that a full dress rehearsal of Chastise took place on the evening of Friday 14 May. However with AJ-J temporarily out of commission David and his crew missed out on this event, as did, apparently, Mick Martin. This was the day that the final decision to go ahead with Chastise was taken. On that Friday morning, a signal was received in London from the Joint Chiefs of Staff who had met the previous evening in Washington, where they were accompanying Churchill on his high level visit to the USA. The way things worked in wartime, it was a further 24 hours before this was transmitted to the people who were to carry out the operation, waiting at Scampton. The Assistant Chief of Air Staff (Operations) in London, Air Vice Marshal Norman Bottomley, had to tell Bomber Command at High Wycombe, who had to tell Cochrane and Satterly at No.5 Group Headquarters at Grantham. The signal was received at Grantham at 0900 on Saturday 15 May, whereupon Satterly took the handwritten draft order from his safe and arranged for it to be typed ready for distribution. While Satterly was doing this, Cochrane flew to Scampton to tell Whitworth and Gibson. He arrived in the early afternoon and left to return to Grantham at about 1600, taking Gibson with him. Meanwhile Barnes Wallis had arrived at Scampton in a Wellington, piloted by Vickers test pilot Matt Summers. By 1800, Gibson was back at Scampton and at a meeting in Whitworth's house he and Wallis began the process of briefing the crews by calling in four of the key personnel: Maudslay and Young, the two flight commanders, Hopgood, who would act as Gibson's deputy at the Möhne, and Flt Lt Bob Hay, Martin's bomb aimer, who was the squadron 'Bombing Leader' (Every squadron had a 'leader' for the specialist jobs of bomb aimer, navigator, signals and gunner: their job was to act as liaison between their colleagues and the squadron management on any issues that came up.).

By now, on the evening of the Saturday, the sense of anticipation must have reached fever pitch. Across the airfield some of the Lancasters were already being 'bombed up' with the special 'stores'. The fact that Maudslay, Young, Hopgood and Hay had been called to a meeting would hardly have gone unnoticed.

No. 617 SQUADRON. NIGHT FLYING PROGRAMME 16.5.43.

No.	/O.	Captain.	F/Engr.	Navigator.	W/Optr.	A/Bomber.	Front Gunner.	Rear Gunner.
1.	G.	W/CDR. GIBSON.	SGT. PULFORD.	F/O. TAERUL.	F/LT. HUTCHISON.	/O. SPAFFORD.	F/SGT. DEERING.	F/LT. TREVOR-ROAR.
2.	M.	F/LT. HOPGOOD.	SGT. BRENNAN.	F/O. EARNSHAW.	SGT. MINCHIN.	F/SGT. FRASER.	/O. GREGORY.	/O. BURCHER.
3.	P.	F/LT. MARTIN.	/O. WHITTAKER.	F/LT. LEGGO.	F/O. CHAMBERS.	F/LT. HAY.	S/O. FOXLEE.	F/SGT. SIMPSON.
4.	J.	S/LDR. YOUNG.	SGT. HORSFALL.	SGT. ROBERTS.	SGT. NICHOLS.	F/O. MacCAUSLAND.	SGT. YEO.	SGT. IBBOTSON.
5.	L.	F/LT. MALTBY.	SGT. HATTON.	SGT. NICHOLSON.	SGT. STONE.	P/O. FORT.	SGT. HILL.	SGT. SIMMONDS.
6.	Z.	F/LT. SHANNON.	SGT. HENDERSON.	F/O. WALKER.	F/O. GOODALE.	F/SGT. SUMPTER.	SGT. JAGGER.	/O. BUCKLEY.
7.	B.	S/LDR. MAUDSLAY.	SGT. MARRIOTT.	F/O. URQUHART.	SGT. COTTAM.	/O. FULLER.	F/O. TYTHERLEIGH	SGT. BURROWS.
8.	N.	F/LT. ASTELL.	SGT. KINNEAR.	/O. WILE.	SGT. GARSHOWITZ.	F/O. HOPKINSON.	SGT. GARBES.	SGT. BOLITHO.
9.	.	/O. KNIGHT.	SGT. GRAYSTON.	F/O. HOBDAY.	F/SGT. KELLOW.	F/O. JOHNSON.	SGT. SUTHERLAND.	SGT. O'BRIEN.
10.	E.	F/LT. MUNRO.	SGT. APPLEBY.	F/O. RUMBLES.	SGT. WEAGLON.	SGT. CLAY.	SGT. HOWARTH.	F/SGT. WEEKS.
11.	Q.	F/LT. McCARTHY.	SGT. RATCLIFFE.	F/SGT. McLEAN.	SGT. EATON.	SGT. JOHNSON.	SGT. BATSON.	F/O. RODGER.
12.	H.	/O. RICE.	SGT. SMITH.	F/O. MacFARLANE.	SGT. GOWRIE.	F/SGT. THRASHER.	SGT. MAYNARD.	SGT. BURNS.
13.	K.	SGT. BYERS.	SGT. TAYLOR.	/O. WARNER.	SGT. WILKINSON.	SGT. WHITAKER.	SGT. JARVIE.	SGT. McDOWELL.
14.	E.	F/LT. BARLOW.	SGT. WILLIS.	F/O. BURGESS.	P/O. WILLIAMS.	SGT. GILLESPIE.	P/O. GLINZ.	SGT. LIDDELL.
15.	C.	F/O. OTTLEY.	SGT. MARSDEN.	F/O. BARRETT.	SGT. GUTERMAN.	F/SGT. JOHNSON.	SGT. TEES.	SGT. STRANGE.
16.	S.	/O. BURPEE.	SGT. PEGLER.	SGT. JAYE.	/O. WELLER.	SGT. ARTHUR.	SGT. LONG.	F/SGT. BRADY.
17.	O.	F/SGT. TOWNSEND.	SGT. POWELL.	/O. HOWARD.	F/SGT. CHALMERS.	SGT. FRANKLIN.	SGT. WEBB.	SGT. WILKINSON.
18.	F.	F/SGT. BROWN.	SGT. FENERON.	SGT. HEAL.	SGT. HEWSTONE.	SGT. OANCIA.	SGT. ALLATSON.	F/SGT. McDONALD.
19.	Y.	F/SGT. ANDERSON.	SGT. PATERSON.	SGT. NUGENT.	SGT. BICKLE.	SGT. GREEN.	SGT. EWAN.	SGT. BUCK.

H1.

Battle order for Operation Chastise, called 'Night Flying Programme' for security reasons. The aircraft piloted by Hopgood, Young, Maudslay, Astell, Byers, Barlow, Ottley and Burpee did not return. Only three of the 56 airmen in these eight crews survived.

It was in adjutant Harry Humphries's office the next morning that the battle order for Chastise was prepared. Humphries was in his office early, even though it was a Sunday, and Gibson arrived at about 0900. He told Humphries that at last the squadron was going to war, but he didn't want 'the world' to know about it. He instructed him to make out a battle order but to title it 'Night Flying Programme', and then gave him the crew details and the code orders.

The typed version of the 'Night Flying Programme' is on display at Grantham Museum, along with some of Humphries' other papers. The 19 crews are listed in order of the 'waves' to which they had been assigned, not the order of take-off. The first wave consisted of three groups of three: Gibson, Hopgood and Martin; Young, Maltby and Shannon; Maudslay, Astell and Knight. These were the nine aircraft scheduled to attack the Möhne Dam, and then move on to the Eder. They were to take off in three groups at 2139, 2147 and 2159. The second wave of five – Barlow, Munro, Byers, Rice and McCarthy – were

The Other Ranks Mess at RAF Scampton. The briefing for Operation Chastise took place in the large room on the first floor, to the left of the main door. Apart from its pitched roof, the building looks much as it did in 1943.

PHOTO: CHARLES FOSTER

assigned the Sorpe Dam as their first target, and were supposed to start taking off singly at one minute intervals, 11 minutes before Gibson's group. The remaining five crews – Otley, Burpee, Brown, Townsend and Anderson – made up a mobile reserve and would take off after midnight.

The order roughly followed the skills levels and results that the crews had achieved during practice. David, already widely respected as a good pilot, had proved that he could manage the sustained low-level flying with ease. His crew, all but one of them novices, had also acquitted themselves well in the practice runs, with John Fort proving himself to be a steady and accurate bomb aimer. Some detailed record sheets for the training survive in the archives and show that for instance in the week ending 8 April 1942 David's crew flew three exercises, totalling 12 hours 30 minutes for that week (having flown 14 hours 30 minutes training up to that week). They had dropped 41 practice bombs with an average error of 41 yards.[50]

With the battle order typed up, the 19 pilots and 19 navigators were called to a briefing at about midday, when they were told their targets by both Gibson and Wallis. It is not difficult to imagine the sense of

50 AIR 14/842

nervous anticipation young Vivian Nicholson must have felt. One of the youngest in the room, at only 20, and certainly the only one on his first operation, he would have expected to see his squadron commander and perhaps someone important from Group Headquarters. The white-haired civilian scientist must have been a bit of a surprise. However, Wallis was a fluent and enthusiastic speaker and his detailed knowledge and passion impressed all who heard him.

We know a lot about what Vivian did later that day because his navigator's log has been preserved at Scampton – a model of how such a document should have been compiled, according to John Sweetman. We can guess that Vivian started filling in the form soon after the briefing. His neat handwriting records that he had checked his watch at 1500 GMT (1700 in actual time, with the double summer time in use during the war). The watch was correct and losing 1/4 secs/hour. They were going to fly aircraft number ED906, letter J. He lists the personnel on board: 'Captain: F/L Maltby D.F.C.; Navigator: Sgt Nicholson; F/E: Sgt Hatton; Crew: P/O Fort B/A, Sgt Stone W/OP, Sgt Hill F/GR, Sgt Simmonds R/GR'. He records the orders – 'take-off 2148, Enemy Coast – Fuse missile. IFF! Code! Nav Lights!' These are the tasks to be done after they had crossed the North Sea – the bomb has to be fused, and the Identification Friend or Foe (IFF) system turned off. The navigation lights should have been turned off shortly after take-off. He also wrote down the words 'Lister 880'. Quite why, we can't now be sure, since the Lister Dam was the fourth target that night and was not bombed by any of the crews. Is the ' mark a symbol for feet? Were they told verbally that there were two towers on the Lister Dam approximately 880 ft apart? Wallis had been led to believe that this secondary target did have two towers 886 ft apart, but this was actually incorrect, as the dam actually had just one tower. The official orders for the crew of AJ-J, however, were to attack Target X, the Möhne, and go on to Target Y, the Eder, if it had already been breached. It seems doubtful that they would ever have got to the Lister.

The briefing was held in the first floor room of the Junior Ranks Mess at Scampton. (The outside of the building is used in the 1955 film, and an accurate reproduction of the room was built for the interior scenes.) At some point in the afternoon, according to Sweetman, bomb aimers and gunners were brought into the picture, with small groups clustered around the models, noting details which would be relevant.

At 1800 the general briefing began. As well as the 133 aircrew sitting on benches in front of a dais holding Gibson, other senior officers and Wallis, there was a civilian interloper by the name of Herbert Jeffree, a scientist at Vickers who worked for Wallis. He bluffed his way past the RAF policeman standing as security at the door with a pass that had given him authority to attend the tests at RAF Manston and Reculver. Gibson spoke first, and then introduced Wallis who described the weapon, how it had been developed and the arguments for attacking the German dams. His arguments that the loss of the dams would lead to the curtailment of industrial production for a very long time are still well remembered by those who heard him. Fred Sutherland, front gunner in Les Knight's crew, told me:

> I remember the briefing quite well because we had waited for weeks to find out what we were doing and where we were going. The pilots, navigators, and, I think, the bomb aimers had a pre-briefing in the afternoon. The models of the dams, the pictures and maps were all set up in the room under guard. No person was allowed to enter. I remember seeing the targets for the first time and knowing that this was going to be really touch and go. Gibson ended his speech by saying: 'Well chaps if you don't do it tonight you will be going back tomorrow night to finish it off.' All the speakers concentrated on the importance of the dams and the water to the German war effort.[51]

Cochrane spoke after Wallis, briefly emphasising the 'historic' nature of the operation. He ended his remarks by saying that the raid might do a lot of damage but that they might never read about it in the news. 'It may be a secret until after the war. So don't think that you are going to get your pictures in the papers.' Cochrane may have thought that there might be little publicity, but some people at the Air Ministry had other ideas. The Director of Bombing Operations at the Air Ministry, Air Cdre Sidney Bufton, had already devised a plan for press communiqués after the raid.

Cochrane was followed by Gibson again, who repeated the details of the three waves that he had already given the pilots and navigators. During the discussion that followed Herbert Jeffree, the interloper, piped up to say that it might be dangerous to return with an unused but fused mine.

---

51   Fred Sutherland, email to author, 13 August 2007

After the briefing, at about 1930, the crews went off for their meal – the traditional eggs and bacon, with an extra egg for anyone flying that night. The WAAFs who worked in the separate messes for the officers and sergeants could not help noticing the extra rations, and were now in on the secret that the operation was on.

After the meal the nervousness began to kick in. With up to two hours to wait before their departure some crews went out to their aircraft early and went through their rituals. There was a lot of urinating on wheels, walking twice round aircraft, and chalking messages on mines. Some suffered premonitions that they would not return – Hopgood told Shannon that he knew he wouldn't get back.

Then there were the mascots, the charms that would keep them safe. Micky Martin always carried a small toy koala bear. Gibson wore a German Mae West inflatable lifejacket he had acquired near the beginning of the war. According to Harry Humphries, David always took his field service hat on missions.[52] This 'fore and aft' hat was so old and stained with oil and grease that it may have been the one he was given when he first joined up. Unusually for an officer, he preferred to wear this style of hat, rather than the peaked cap. He can be seen in it in the formal squadron photos in his 97 Squadron days, the ones taken later at 617 Squadron, and even on the day of the King's visit after the raid. Whether this was the same stained one, or a later, cleaner model is impossible to tell.

Four of the five aircraft in the second wave took off first (Joe McCarthy found a fault in his plane and had to transfer to the reserve, which led him to be delayed). It wasn't common for Lancasters to take off in formation but on this occasion they did, Gibson leading Hopgood and Martin down the grass runway into the bright May evening sky. Eight minutes later, at 2147, Young led out the V-Vic with the two Davids just behind, Maltby on the right, Shannon on the left.

Sitting at his desk inside the fuselage, below the Perspex astrodome, with his maps, an air position indicator and the apparatus for the Gee system at hand, Vivian Nicholson sat ready for his first ever operation. The navigator would spend the whole flight making detailed calculations and advising small changes in course and the Gee system was there to help him. Introduced in 1942, Gee sent out pulses from three separate transmitters, located in southern England, which appeared as blips on a screen in front of the navigator. It was designed to make it

---

52 Humphries, *Living with Heroes*, p.34

easier for him to get an accurate fix of the aircraft's position. However, it had limited range and the signal was frequently jammed by the Germans, so it was not always useful. That was certainly the case on the night of the Dams Raid.

Vivian's log records the details of the flight. At 2210, over the Wash, they tested the spotlights set to keep the aircraft at exactly 60 ft during the bombing run. They made landfall accurately over the Scheldt estuary on the Dutch coast at 2312, and the mine was then fused. David had to take 'evasive action' to avoid flak at Rosendaal. At the canal intersection at Beck, Vivian wrote 'Leader turns soon'. He probably meant 'too soon', as Young's aircraft went slightly off course. At 2342, about 15 miles from the Rhine, he noted that his Gee system was now 'jammed something chronic'. They turned again at Dülmen, avoided more flak, 'direct at a/c' at Ludinghausen, and also at Ahlen, and arrived at Target X, the Möhne at 0026. The outward flight had taken 2 hours 32 minutes.

It had been a textbook flight out. Major Alan Thompson, an Army pilot who now conducts tours around Dambuster sites for a travel company, says that he always describes the crew of AJ-J as doing the job exactly as they had been instructed. They stayed low, took evasive action when necessary and hit all their turning points accurately. And, of course, in a few minutes they would drop their mine at the right height, the right distance and the right speed.

But that was to come. For the moment David and the other five crews circled the area above the Möhne, to be joined shortly by Maudslay and Knight. Bill Astell had crashed. He seems to have hesitated at a turning point, then flew into flak and collided with a high tension pylon. His crew included two Canadians, Albert Garshowitz and Frank Garbas, who had grown up together as friends in Hamilton, Ontario and are now buried together in Reichswald Forest Cemetery.[53]

The Möhne Reservoir is the shape of a giant U on its side, the open end facing east, or right. The dam is on the top left part of the curve of the U. Earlier books, including Sweetman's, say that the aircraft approached from the Körbecke bridge at the eastern end, but that is now thought to be wrong. The aircraft attacked by flying straight at the dam from a south-easterly direction, hopping over a small spit of land and quickly getting down to the right height for the last stretch of about

---

53   Frank Garbas's nephew, Paul Morley, has written movingly about the pair and his trip to their grave at www.lancastermuseum.ca

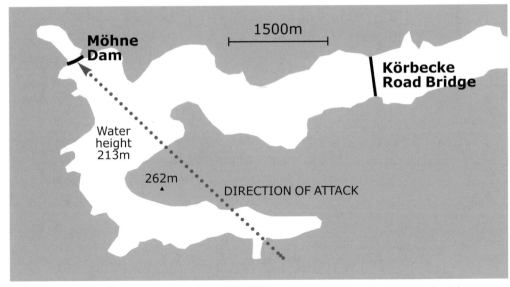

Most earlier accounts of the Dams Raid state that the aircraft that attacked the Möhne Dam came in from above the Körbecke Bridge, turning half right over the small spit of land before flying straight at the dam. It is now thought that they approached from the forested area south east of the lake, flying over the larger spit, before descending for the final attack. MAP DRAWN BY AUTHOR

1,500m. In that last 1,500m the pilot would have to get down to exactly 60 ft and stay level, the flight engineer would maintain the approach speed at 230 mph, and the wireless operator would ensure that the mine was spinning backwards at 500 rpm. Meanwhile the navigator would switch on the spotlights and check that the beams were touching. Flying at 230 mph, the aircraft would cover the 1,500m stretch in about 15 seconds.

It is not always noted that Chastise marked another important innovation in bombing technique. VHF radio sets, previously only fitted to fighter aircraft, were used by bombers for the first time. This meant that crews could talk to each other and therefore be controlled by a leader, or 'master bomber' as they were later to be known.

By the time Young, Maltby and Shannon had got to the dam Gibson had flown over it, without revealing the exact direction of attack, and came through the flak unscathed. He told the others that he 'liked the look of it'. So, just two minutes after this trio arrived, he began his run in. It seemed at first that everything had gone to plan – the mine was spun correctly and was seen to bounce three times. But it did not reach the dam wall, exploding a few yards short. A great plume of water rose up into the air, but the dam held.

Back in Britain, in the operations room at 5 Group headquarters in Grantham, Wallis, Cochrane and other assorted staff had been joined by Air Marshal Sir Arthur Harris himself, who had driven the 120 miles from Bomber Command HQ in High Wycombe. When Gibson's 'Goner 58A' signal was received, indicating an unsuccessful attack, with the mine exploding between 5 and 50 yards short, a sense of gloom descended.

Gibson then called Hopgood into attack. Flt Sgt John Fraser, Hopgood's bomb aimer, later remembered Gibson describing the run-in as a 'piece of cake', which is certainly not what it seemed like to him. (How frightfully understated the slang of that time seems to us today.) As Hopgood crossed the stretch of water towards the dam, the anti-aircraft gunners on it were now ready. His aircraft was hit on one side. The flight engineer shouted a warning, Fraser dropped the mine, knowing that he had done so too late and heard Hopgood screaming 'For Christ's sake get out of here!' Hopgood struggled on, trying to lift the aircraft, and got it up to about 500 ft. The mine bounced over the dam and into the power station on the far side, causing a big explosion and a fire. Fraser, Minchin and Burcher, baled out but Minchin, already injured, did not survive the parachute drop. Hopgood and the other three died in the crash. Burcher and Fraser were captured. Fraser went back to Canada after the war and later he would name his first son John Hopgood Fraser after the pilot who had kept his aircraft aloft long enough to save his life.

The next few minutes were surely what earned Gibson his Victoria Cross, as he called up Martin to attack. In the words of John Sweetman, 'Gibson's leadership and Martin's courage ensured that the operation would not disintegrate.' Gibson flew slightly ahead of Martin on his starboard side, in the hope that the gunners would be distracted. However, something went wrong with Martin's mine: it veered off leftwards and exploded near the southern shore of the lake. Its casing may have been damaged when it was dropped accidentally onto the hard standing at Scampton that morning, or, perhaps, Martin hadn't got the aircraft exactly level as it was released.

Sqn Ldr Melvin Young, whose rowing Blue from Oxford may have helped him survive the two ditchings at sea which earned him the nickname 'Dinghy', was next. This time, Gibson flew across the defences on the far side of the dam wall, and Martin came in on the starboard side. Young was accurate in his approach, and his bomb aimer, Flg Off Vincent MacCausland, dropped the mine accurately. It bounced three times, hit the dam and seemed to explode while it was in contact with it, but, as the tumult subsided, there was no obvious breach.

As they waited, knowing they were next in, David and his crew continued to circle north of the dam, along with the aircraft of Shannon, Maudslay and Knight. Vivian Nicholson noted 'flak none too light'. Gibson told David to go ahead at 0048, and Vivian wrote, 'received OK' as they started the approach. This time, three Lancasters flew towards the target. Gibson on David's starboard side, Martin over to port.

Anthony Stone checked the spinning mine, John Fort lay flat on his stomach in the front fuselage, waiting, with Vic Hill's feet planted in their stirrups over his head. As they came over the spit of land, Vivian turned on the spotlights and peered out of the starboard blister at the beams, calling, 'Down, down' as their lights came closer and closer. Up in the cockpit, in the left-hand seat, David adjusted the height and kept the aircraft level while, next to him, Bill Hatton watched the speed and moved the throttles. As they approached the dam wall, David suddenly realised that from this close he could see a small breach had occurred in the centre and that there was crumbling along the crown. Young's mine had been successful after all! In a last second change of plan he veered slightly to port but stayed dead level as John Fort steadied himself to press the release. The mine bounced four times and struck the wall. Over the dam they flew, now turning hard left, Harold Simmonds in the rear turret firing on the gun emplacements that were still active.

The dam was protected by a flak battery in each of the two sluice towers and another in the wall. In the northern tower was a gunner called Unteroffizier Karl Schütte, who later gave an account of the night's proceedings. In fact the flak guns in the north tower had jammed and Karl Schütte and his comrades were reduced to shooting at David's plane with rifles. The gun on the parapet was still firing, however. There are two slightly different versions of his account. One says:

During the fourth attack, our gun failed after a premature explosion in the barrel. We bashed away with all our strength trying to clear the jam with a hammer and a metal spike but it was no good. When it came to the fifth attack we did what we'd so often done in training – let loose with our carbines. There was just one flak gun on the road still firing at the aircraft – now they had it all their own way. There was a muffled explosion and when the spray had cleared a bit I had a quick look over the parapet down at the dam wall and shouted, 'The wall's had it.' The gunners didn't want to believe it at first but the breach got visibly bigger.[54]

The other version says:

Then a fifth plane started its attack. Only the gun in the lower wall was still firing. The machine neared the wall at an incredible speed; they now had an easy game – I could almost touch it, yet I think even today I can see the outline of the pilot.[55]

It wasn't yet obvious whether the attack had been successful so at 0050 Antony Stone, doing his job correctly, radioed 'Goner 78A' back to Grantham. ('Goner' meant a successful attack, '7' an explosion in contact with the dam, '8' no apparent breach, 'A' the target was the Möhne.)

David said afterwards that, 'our load sent up water and mud to a height of a 1,000 ft. The spout of water was silhouetted against the moon. It rose with tremendous speed and then gently fell back. You could see the shock wave at the base of the jet.'[56] 'Bomb dropped. Wizard.' was what Vivian noted immediately in his log.

The lake began to calm down again and Gibson called Shannon into the attack. But as Shannon began to line up the circling crews realised that the dam had indeed been broken. David's mine, dropped to the left of Young's, had been pulled towards it by the flow of water before it exploded and caused a second breach. (In the end the two breaches would be joined together by the force of escaping water to make a single breach some 76m wide.) It was 0056, a full six minutes after David's attack when the breach was confirmed. Gibson's wireless operator, Flt Lt Bob Hutchison, quickly tapped out the code word 'Nigger' and sent it back to Grantham.

So who actually broke the dam, Young or Maltby? As children, we

---

54 Helmuth Euler, *The Dams Raid through the Lens*, After the Battle, 2001, p.68
55 Alan Cooper, *The Men Who Breached the Dams*, Airlife 2002, p.88
56 *Daily Mail*, 18 May 1943, cited in Sweetman, *Dambusters Raid*, p.166. (This quote is attributed in the newspaper article to an anonymous flight lieutenant, but Sweetman is convinced that the actual source is Maltby.)

were always told that David dropped the bomb that caused the breach. This impression is certainly given in the Gibson and Brickhill books and the 1955 film. In *Enemy Coast Ahead*, Gibson wrote that when Melvin Young said, 'I think I've done it, I've broken it', he told him he hadn't.[57] To David's credit, he never claimed the breach as entirely his work – his answer to the debriefing questionnaire quite clearly states that as he attacked he saw the small breach made by Young , and that's why he turned slightly to port. Whether Young's small breach on its own would have resulted in a complete collapse of the dam is something that will never be known. The dam was immensely strong and it may well have needed two explosions to break it. What is quite clear is that only two mines out of the five were dropped correctly, and between them they broke the dam. Wallis's calculations were proven to be good.

✳ ✳ ✳

The operations room at Grantham, in the basement of a large house called St Vincent's on the edge of the town, was accurately reproduced in the 1955 film. It was a long narrow room, with a raised platform down one side where the chief signals officer, Wg Cdr Wally Dunn, sat anxiously with a telephone plugged into the W/T Morse code receiver. Dunn could read Morse as quickly as any wireless operator and translated each message immediately to the group clustered in front of him, expectantly waiting.

There are two different versions of the timings of the four 'Goner' messages that were received from the Möhne. Both say that the first was Gibson's at 0037. and that then, for some reason, Young's arrived next at 0050, causing consternation amongst Satterly, Cochrane and others who knew the bombing order. This implied that only two of the first four aircraft had go through, and spelled disaster.

Wallis paced up and down, 'having kittens' according to Cochrane afterwards. Gibson's 'Goner' signal caused him to mutter, 'No, it's no good.' Young's made him bury his head in his hands. At 0050, when Antony Stone sent AJ-J's message, desperation set in, compounded by the late arrival at 0051 of Martin's. (The second version of the signal log shows that AJ-J's message was received at 0055, after Martin's was received at 0053.) Whichever order the signals were received in, back at Grantham it was thought that five aircraft had apparently failed.

57 Gibson, *Enemy Coast Ahead*, p.291

Nothing more was heard for perhaps as long as five minutes. But then, suddenly, at 0056, the 'Nigger' signal was received, and then confirmed.

Scenes of jubilation followed. Wallis leapt into the air, arms aloft. As Harris shook his hand, everyone who heard him remembers the words: 'Wallis, I didn't believe a word you said when you came to see me. But now you could sell me a pink elephant.'

At the Möhne the seven aircraft still aloft circled for a short while, chattering amongst themselves on the VHF sets. Then Gibson, conscious that they had only attacked the first of the night's targets, ordered the three that had still not bombed, Shannon, Maudslay and Knight, to accompany him and Young to the Eder. (Young was to act as his deputy if he went down.) He told David and Mick Martin to set course for home. At $0053^1/_2$ according to the meticulous Vivian, AJ-J set a bearing of 280 degrees and headed off. The details are recorded again: turning points at Ahlen and Zutphen, with evasive action taken at Ahlen. They crossed the coast exactly one hour after leaving the Möhne, meeting some flak and searchlights there and with the Gee 'still no dice'. Crossing the North Sea, the Gee rather belatedly became 'faint but workable'. They rose to the giddy height of 1,500 ft, but then, somewhat oddly, descended again to test their spotlights. They crossed the bombing range at Wainfleet in the Wash, and touched down at Scampton at 0311. Martin's aircraft arrived safely eight minutes later.

There to greet them were Leading Aircraftmen Law and Payne.[58] Once the aircraft had been handed over to the groundcrew, David and his colleagues went to stow their kit before meeting the intelligence officers for their debriefing. By the time he bumped into Harry Humphries, Gibson and the Eder dam survivors must also have landed as David was able to give Humphries news of some of the other casualties. Humphries remembers their conversation:

'How was it Dave?' I queried.
'A terrific show, Adj., absolutely terrific. I have never seen anything like it in my life,' he said, then quite bluntly, 'Hoppy's bought it.
'Bought it, when?' I asked.
'Shot down over the target, and I am afraid we have lost several others too,' he answered. He pushed his Mae West viciously into his locker. 'Some didn't even get there and I am sure "Dinghy" Young got into

58 Cooper, *Men Who Breached the Dams*, p.100

trouble, and maybe Henry Maudsley [sic].'

He turned and gave me his usual broad grin. 'We pranged it though, Adj., oh boy did we prang it! Water, water everywhere. "Gibby" was everywhere. How the hell the Jerry gunners missed him I don't know.' He added, 'Did you bury "Nigger" for the Wingco?'

I started, 'I um... to tell you the truth, Dave, I don't know. Why do you ask anyway?'

'Oh it was just worrying Gibby, I know. It just struck me that superstition means nothing anyway, even though I always take this hat with me.'

'This hat' was David's field service or 'fore and aft'. It was a filthy thing, covered in oil and grease but he would not be separated from that hat, even on parade. 'Well, see you later over a beer,' he said and shouted to the rest of his crew, 'so long sprogs, thanks for coming.'[59]

Although Humphries says this conversation happened soon after landing, it is more likely that it occurred after the crews had been debriefed, with an intelligence officer giving all the pilots a questionnaire and recording their comments. In it, David described how he saw a breach in the centre of the dam before attacking, and went to port and made a contact. His mine was spun correctly and bounced three times. His main criticism was that the aircraft were exposed by being against the moon as they made their attack.

By 0400, Harris, Cochrane and Wallis had all left Grantham for Scampton, and personally greeted some of the later arrivals. The last aircraft to get back – at 0615 – was piloted by Bill Townsend, who didn't recognise Harris in his Air Chief Marshal's uniform and pushed past him rather abruptly.

By then, the knowledge of who had not survived must have begun to sink in. David had seen Hopgood shot down, and would have known that Astell had never got as far as the target. With Young and Maudslay failing to make it back from the Eder, four of the elite nine in the first wave had gone. From the second and third waves, another four crews – Barlow, Byers, Ottley and Burpee – had been lost. Like David, Lewis Burpee had a pregnant wife waiting at home.

It is not certain, but it's unlikely that, in the dawn light, David travelled the 30 miles back to Woodhall Spa to see his own pregnant wife. (As Nina had been at her parents' house in Kent earlier in the week, she

---

59 Humphries, *Living with Heroes*, p.44

might anyway not have been in Woodhall at all.) By all accounts David was an enthusiastic partygoer and would have joined in the general merriment that ensued amongst many of the survivors. The mess bars were reopened, and Gp Capt Whitworth's house became the scene of an impromptu party, culminating in a conga dance around his house and the seizing of his pyjamas as a trophy. In any event, David was certainly at Scampton some time in the morning, since he is in the photograph taken outside the officers mess. When this was taken many of those photographed were apparently somewhat the worse for wear, though it is not too obvious from the picture.

With only eleven of the 19 Lancasters having returned, the airfield seemed a lot quieter. A Tannoy announcement during the morning told everyone on the base what had occurred, but many were more aware of the scale of the losses. At one point Wallis was reported to be in tears, devastated by the fact that 56 young men were missing. (At that stage no one knew that three had survived and been captured as prisoners of war.) Although the last scene of the 1955 film, where Gibson and Wallis have a conversation which ends with Gibson saying, 'I have some letters to write', is fictionalised it bears some, but not complete, resemblance to the truth. It was Humphries and Sgt Heveron who spent much of the morning sending telegrams to the next of kin. In the afternoon, they were interrupted in this work by Gibson, bearing the news that all 900 aircrew and groundcrew were to be sent on leave the next day. The process of drafting letters to the next of kin didn't begin until Tuesday 18 May, after the leave had begun.

By that time, the world had been informed of the scale of the achievement. BBC radio had broadcast the Air Ministry communiqué at lunchtime on the Monday. (The same communiqué was read again for the 1955 film by the wartime BBC announcer Frank Phillips, where, as the words die away, we see a moving set of shots including the survivors eating breakfast, the empty chairs in the mess, Dinghy Young's Oxford oar on the wall and an alarm clock ticking away, its hands showing the time as just after 6am. It's a beautiful, understated piece of visual and sound editing, and another time when the scriptwriter and director's decisions to vary the historical record slightly by bringing the broadcast forward in time by several hours is fully justified.)

This is London. The Air Ministry has just issued the following commu-

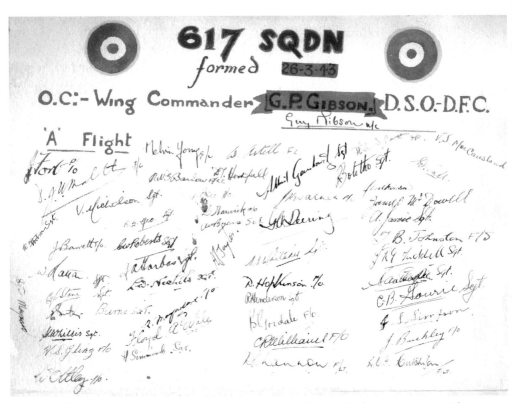

Harry Humphries pinned up two large sheets of paper in the crew room, with the aim of collecting signatures of all the aircrew in 617 Squadron. Most of A Flight signed up including six of the crew of AJ-J. Victor Hill didn't sign, which suggests that the rest added their names before he joined the crew on 7 May.

PHOTO: LINCOLNSHIRE COUNTY COUNCIL, GRANTHAM MUSEUM

niqué. In the early hours of this morning, a force of Lancasters of Bomber Command led by Wing Cdr G P Gibson DSO DFC attacked with mines the dams of the Möhne and Sorpe reservoirs. These control over two-thirds of the water storage capacity of the Ruhr basin. Reconnaissance later established that the Möhne dam had been breached over a length of one hundred yards, and that the power station below had been swept away. The Eder dam, which controls the headwaters of the Weser and Fulde valleys and operates several power stations, was also attacked and reported as breached. Photographs show the river below the dam in full flood. The attacks were pressed home from a very low level with great determination and coolness in the face of fierce resistance. Eight of the Lancasters are missing.

A group of Dams Raid survivors outside the Officers Mess on the morning of 17 May 1943. As most had been drinking hard since soon after they landed they look surprisingly spruce. John Fort is on the extreme right in the front row, David Maltby second from right in the second row. PHOTO: IWM/HU91948

On the Tuesday, every paper carried the full story as its lead. David found time to let his family know that he had been involved. He sent a telegram to his uncle, Aubrey Hatfeild, who had been a pilot in the RFC in the First World War: 'We let the plug out!' In his diary, Ettrick recorded that David had 'returned first from the Moehne Dam'.

Also on the Tuesday, David was promoted to Squadron Leader, and given command of A Flight. In effect he was now second in command of 617 Squadron. It must have been a bitter sweet moment because five out of the ten crews in the Flight had been lost on the raid. (These were the crews led by Young, the Flight Commander, Astell, Barlow, Ottley and Byers.) Many of these had written their names on the signature sheets posted by Harry Humphries in the crew room. He had been hoping to get a complete record of all the men in the squadron, but so many were now missing that instead he quietly stowed the sheets away. They are now in the Grantham Museum.

We know that David, like many members of Bomber Command, certainly did not glory in the fact that his work often resulted in the deaths

of others. The Dams Raid did cause a large loss of life, although perhaps not as severe as had been initially thought. The official German
casualty figures show that 1,294 people died as a result of the Möhne
Dam's collapse, with 47 more losing their lives in the Eder valley. Of
the dead and missing in the Möhne area 749 were listed as 'foreigners',
of whom 493 were Ukrainian women labourers, ordered back to their
camp for safety when the air raid warnings sounded.

Chapter 8

∗

After the Dams Raid

The RAF Museum in Hendon has a file of press cuttings about Operation Chastise, all neatly pasted into what advertising agencies call a 'guard book'. This is a large format clothbound book with leaves made of stiff grey paper, and is designed to keep a permanent record of newspaper and magazine advertising. Turning over the pages you get a real idea of the impact that the Dams Raid must have made at the time. By May 1943, the British people were starting to think that the war was going their way – the Allies had had a run of success over the previous few months with El Alamein in November 1942 and the final Soviet victory in Stalingrad in February 1943 particularly seen as great triumphs. After Alamein, Churchill once more found words which seemed to capture the mood: 'this is not the end, it is not even the beginning of the end. But it is, perhaps, the end of the beginning.'

Now, a day or two after news had reached Britain of the final Allied victory in Tunisia, which meant that plans for the invasion of Sicily and then Italy could go ahead, this daring raid on the dams in the Ruhr valleys captured the imagination. Nowadays we would call the press and public relations operation mounted by the Air Ministry and the Ministry of Information 'spin', with all the pejorative overtones that that implies, but there is no doubt that the press was given substantial help in the production of their stories, including the release of the dramatic reconnaissance photographs. Of course in war time, with no opportunity to check material and with the only foreign reports coming from neutral Switzerland, Sweden and Spain, it is completely understandable that the press should carry what the official sources wanted them to say.

This would explain why some of the details were either wrong or based on speculation. The *Daily Telegraph*, for instance, informed its

Photograph of the Möhne Dam taken by RAF reconnaisance aircraft the day after Operation Chastise. The barrage balloons were not present when the raid took place.

readers that 'three key dams' had been blown up, while the *Daily Mirror* was more sensationalist, with a headline reading 'Huns get a flood blitz: torrent rages along Ruhr'. The *Daily Mail* ran a headline over its photographs: 'The Smash-Up: RAF Picture Testifies to Perfect Bombing'. Its story went on: 'Two mighty walls of water were last night rolling irresistibly down the Ruhr and Eder valleys. Railway bridges, power stations, factories, whole villages and built-up areas were being swept away.'

Flicking through the guard book, I saw how the coverage lasted for days, fed by further information coming from the Air Ministry, as the floods spread further and further down the valleys. 'Havoc spreads hour by hour' one paper recorded, and there was speculation that the third dam might burst at any moment. The weekly magazines got in on the act at the end of the week, and the following week as well, with one, the *Illustrated London News,* carrying an extraordinary double page spread 'artist's impression' of 'how the raid was carried out'. This was drawn by no less a person than the 'celebrated aviation artist' Captain

Bryan de Grineau 'from information given by the Air Ministry'. In it, a Lancaster is shown flying along the length of the Möhne Dam, not directly towards it, which is what actually happened. The ostensible way in which the operation was carried out was explained thus:

> The bomber crews' tricky task was to drop 1,500 lb mines in a confined area inside the torpedo net... in the centre of the dam, where the current would draw them down towards the sluice gates and explode them there. The attack had to be made with perfect coolness, and the mines dropped from a height of sometimes less than 100ft.

Poor Captain de Grineau and his editors were being spun a complete fabrication. This was a cover story, dreamed up by the Air Ministry for public consumption. Gibson was to describe the same fictional technique on his later US and Canadian lecture tour. The intelligence services weren't to know that concealing the details of the mine was futile: the Germans had already recovered an unexploded Upkeep mine (from the crashed aircraft of Flt Lt Barlow) and were busy working out its secrets even as these articles were appearing in the press.

The King and Queen's visit to Scampton ten days after the raid (which was carefully described as 'an air station in the north of England') and the list of decorations which accompanied it prompted another round of press interest. This brought about the first use of the word 'dam-buster', which appears on the day of the royal visit, 27 May 1943, in a small headline in the *Daily Mirror:* 'Dam-buster Gibson to get V.C.' The *Mirror* (perhaps the same anonymous sub-editor on another evening shift?) was obviously quite pleased with its new word, as it was used a couple of times again in the week following, and other papers such as the *Daily Sketch* soon followed suit.

It wasn't just the national and international press who covered the raid. Local papers also became involved. The arrival home on leave of AJ-J's flight engineer, Bill Hatton, was noted by the *Wakefield Express* under the heading 'A Wakefield Hero'. Readers were informed that he had taken part 'in the great raid on the German dams'.

When it came out, the list of decorations was pretty astonishing. Of the 77 airmen who returned from the raid, 34 were awarded an honour of one sort or another, with Guy Gibson receiving the highest possible award for bravery, the Victoria Cross. More than half the personnel in the crews who succeeded in both bombing and getting home safely were decorated. (Two crews had to make an early return after their aircraft were damaged on the outward flight.)

Amongst those decorated were three crew members from AJ-J. Like all the crews who dropped their mines successfully, the pilot, navigator and bomb aimer were decorated. A strict pecking order was followed: officer pilots were awarded a Distinguished Service Order (DSO), the two non-commissioned pilots got the equivalent CGM – the Conspicuous Gallantry Medal (Flying). All the other officers got Distinguished Flying Crosses (DFC), while the other sergeants and flight sergeants got Distinguished Flying Medals (DFM).

There is something of a mystery as to why the medals were divided out in this way. The only aircraft where all seven members were decorated was Gibson's. That's understandable enough, but why six of Bill Townsend's crew (all except the poor old flight engineer) got medals is not at all clear. They had a difficult enough flight, arriving back last of all, and were the only crew who bombed the Ennepe Dam – but it didn't breach. When front gunner Sgt Douglas Webb got a telegram about his medal, he thought at first it was a practical joke. (Of all the Operation Chastise survivors Doug Webb had one of the most remarkable postwar careers. He went back to working in Fleet Street as a photographer and then branched out into film stills and 'glamour' work. It was while doing this work that he took the first nude pictures of the celebrated model and actress Pamela Green, while she was still a schoolgirl. In the 1950s and 60s she made a career out of glamour work, culminating in the naturist picture *Naked as Nature Intended*. Her straight acting career included the 1960 Michael Powell film *Peeping Tom* where the moderately explicit shots of her got local watch committees in a fuss. Doug and Pamela's relationship was more than professional – they were eventually married in 1967. They later retired to the Isle of Wight, where she still lives after his death in 1996.)

So, David Maltby was awarded a DSO to add to the DFC he had received nine months before, while John Fort got a DFC and Vivian Nicholson a DFM. The draft citations make interesting reading, as well as being riddled with typing errors. (The strain of preparing 34 citations must have told on the typist, as these are not the only ones that occurred.) Vivian is called 'Victor' (although as his medal was engraved

Sgt V Nicholson, perhaps this didn't matter too much). David's middle name is spelt 'Hatfield', a common error, and he is wrongly allocated 28 operations, when Chastise was actually his 29th. John Fort's rank varies between Pilot Officer and Flying Officer in the course of two pages. His promotion, when it came through later, was backdated to 15 March 1943, so technically the higher rank is correct. What is astonishing are the hours flown and the number of operations. Here it is in black and white: Vivian had flown operational hours of 5 hours and 40 minutes in just one operation; John for 9 hours and 40 minutes in two. They were, by far, the most inexperienced of the 34 decorated aircrew in 617 Squadron, and Vivian was probably the youngest.

The recommendation reads:

PARTICULARS OF MERITORIOUS SERVICE
Flight Lieutenant Maltby was Captain, Sergeant Nicholson was Navigator and Pilot Officer Fort was Air Bomber of an aircraft which was detailed to attack the Mohne Dam. By an extremely high standard of crew co-operation, and by showing the greatest sense of duty in the face of heavy opposition and other difficulties, this crew succeeded in making the final breach in the Mohne Dam.

I strongly recommend the immediate award of the Distinguished Service Order to F/Lt. Maltby, and the Distinguished Flying Cross to P/O. Fort, and of the Distinguished Flying Medal to Sgt. Nicholson.

The recommendations were signed by Whitworth. Over the page Cochrane and Harris added their signatures concurring in the awards.

When the King and Queen came to Scampton, each crew was lined up behind their captain, who stood smartly to attention, toecaps touching a white line painted on the grass. Gibson introduced the King to each of the pilots. Some sources[60] say that the pilots each then introduced the rest of his crew, but this is at odds with what can be seen from the few seconds shown on the contemporary newsreels and the accounts of Len Sumpter and Fred Sutherland, who said that they did not.[61] An official RAF photographer recorded the scene, and shot some of the pictures in colour. When you are so used to seeing war time pictures in black and white the rich Kodachrome process is almost shockingly bright.

60 Sweetman, *Dambusters Raid*, p.244; Morris, *Guy Gibson*, p.179
61 Bishop, *Bomber Boys*, p.188; John Sweetman, David Coward and Gary Johnstone, *The Dambusters*, Time Warner, 2003, p.160

Scampton, 27 May 1943. The crews were presented to the King and Queen in their bombing order. so David Shannon came immediately after David Maltby, whose pockets are bulging with a tobacco pouch and other smoking equipment. Vivian Nicholson can be seen over Shannon's shoulder.

PHOTOS: IWM CH9929/CH9953

Most of the shots show the King and Queen talking to the pilots. In the one of Shannon, Vivian Nicholson can be seen in the distance, eyes front, at attention behind David. In the shot of David himself, the King seems to be asking him a question, and David looks nervous as he gropes for an answer. Curiously, he is still only wearing a Flight Lieutenant's two rings on his sleeve. The inner half-ring indicating his promotion to Squadron Leader ten days previously has not yet been added.

The following day Ettrick wrote to Henry Kendall, the Warden (headmaster) of St Edward's School. He knew him well – as it was his own old school, boys from Hydneye regularly went on to St Edward's. He first congratulated him on the fact that the raid had been led by a St Edward's old boy, ('Floreat St Edward's indeed!') then added: 'You will be doubly interested to know that my David was on the raid too and has been given the D.S.O.' After asking for the news to be passed on to a number of Hydneye old boys at St Edward's he says: 'I certainly feel proud of him, but I think the word "thankful" should have most promi-nence.'

David's promotion to Squadron Leader and role as the Commander of A Flight meant a lot of bureaucratic work, such as planning schedules and countersigning logbooks. On 2 June he took over temporary com-mand of the squadron while Gibson was on leave. The flight authorisa-tion books show that intensive training was going on during this time. Flights averaging about two hours took place almost every day, to famil-iar training locations such as the lake at Uppingham or the bombing ranges at Wainfleet.

On one of these occasions David was able to show off to his old school friend Alan Pegler. David telephoned Alan on Saturday 29 May to tip him off that he would be flying over his family's house at Blyth in north Nottinghamshire. Alan was himself already a qualified pilot at the beginning of the war, and had joined the Fleet Air Arm. However, it was then discovered that he was medically unfit for combat duties, so he had moved into the Royal Observer Corps. It was quickly discovered that his railway enthusiast skills were readily translated into a natural talent for aircraft recognition, and he was soon heavily involved in training other observers.

So it was with great interest that Alan waited to see what would fly

28th May.

Ref. Guy Gibson V.C Hydneye House
1943.

Maltby

My dear Henry.

Flodal' S' Edwards indeed! I
do congratulate you all —

You will be doubly interested to
know that my David was on the raid
too & that he has been given the D.S.O

I wonder if you will kindly pass on the
information to Nicoll, Sayer, Grunside, Bartlett
& B. Brown. They will be thrilled —
I certainly feel proud of him, but I think
the word "thankful" should have most
prominence — I hope all is well with you
Yours Ettrick. G. Maltby.

Letter sent by Ettrick Maltby to Rev Henry Kendall, Warden of St Edward's School.

over his house that day, and he was rewarded by the sight of David and one of his colleagues (probably Bill Divall) flying very low over the Pegler home. He distinctly recalls the unusual shape of the modified Lancasters and was able to take a good photograph of them as they passed overhead. Much to Alan's annoyance, one of his relatives disposed of many of his photographs after the war, amongst them this unique shot.

Meanwhile, there was no word about what Bomber Command planned to do with the squadron. This gave time for the squadron to support Gibson in his growing public relations role. Gibson was sent off to places such as Sheffield, Gloucester and Maidstone to speak at Wings for Victory events. These were special events run by the National Savings organisation to encourage people to save money and thereby combat inflation. According to Angus Calder the propaganda for the schemes was actually 'economic nonsense' since financial institutions always issued bonds which made it quite easy for local committees to meet the monstrous targets that were set them. However, local Wings For Victory Weeks helped to raise morale and made people think that they were directly helping the war effort.[62] So it was that the climax of Gibson's speech during Maidstone's Wings for Victory Week on Saturday 19 June was marked by the sight of four Lancasters, piloted by David Maltby, David Shannon, Mick Martin and Les Munro, 'beating up' the town.

There was also time for more occasional airborne detours to impress friends and relations. The day after David's trip to Maidstone, Sunday 20 June, Ettrick recorded in his diary 'David over Witherdon in a Lancaster'. Since his marriage, and with Nina pregnant, David had obviously not been coming back to Devon so frequently, for Ettrick then writes, 'The last time he was here was Nov. 42'. In fact, he was never to go to Witherdon again. The entry in the Flight Authorisation Book for that day shows that he was flying a low-level cross-country exercise 'Base-Winchester-Somerton-Caldy Island [sic]-Shrewsbury-Base' which took 3 hours 20 minutes. The straight route from Somerton to Caldey Island would have taken him over the edge of Exmoor, so a short diversion over Witherdon would have been entirely possible. On another occasion he took an even shorter deviation to Northamptonshire. His cousin, Frances Bonsey, remembers:

The last time I had a glimpse of David was very shortly before he died. Mum, Aunt Aileen and I were sitting in the garden at Little Houghton when a huge aircraft flew low over us. Aunt Aileen said 'It's David, he'll be back in a minute' and sure enough there he was roaring overhead. We could see him waving and we all waved back.

The day after David's flight over Witherdon, on Monday 21 June, Aileen

---

62 Angus Calder, *The People's War*, Panther, 1972, p.411

Relaxing outside the Officers Mess, sometime after the Dams Raid. Left to right: Les Knight, Geoff Rice, David Maltby, Guy Gibson, David Shannon. Mick Martin, Joe McCarthy. Far right, shading his eyes, is Les Munro.

PHOTO: ALEX BATEMAN

and Ettrick set off for London. They had booked into the Piccadilly Hotel, and had arranged for both David and my mother Jean to stay there as well. They had all been invited to the investiture ceremony the next day at Buckingham Palace, where the 34 aircrew were to get their medals, among them, of course, David, Vivian Nicholson and John Fort.

A special train was organised and Squadron Adjutant Harry Humphries had all his legendary administrative skills tested to the limit getting the boisterous aircrew to the station, onto the train and up to London without a major incident. The news that A V Roe Ltd had organised a dinner for the evening after the investiture added to the determination of many to start the party a day early, so copious amounts of alcohol were brought along to ensure that the trip was well lubricated.

David seems to have been one of the ringleaders in the antics that followed. According to Humphries, he started by removing the small brass badges saying 'VR' for Volunteer Reserve from the lapels of a young Pilot Officer from the RAF's Railway Transport Office.

At Grantham
Station, boarding
the train to London
for the investiture.
David Maltby on
the extreme left.
John Fort on
platform edge, next
to the engine
footplate.

Apparently the Air Ministry had decreed that these were no longer to be worn. 'You won't be needing these, old boy and may I add you're lucky it's not your trousers,' Humphries quotes him as saying. (Strangely, David is himself wearing his own VR badges in the picture of him meeting the King less than a month before, so this ruling must have only just been made.) The loss of trousers became a theme for the journey. The wireless operator in Shannon's crew, Brian Goodale, had his removed while drinking and playing cards with the 'bloods'. He turned up in his underpants in the compartment where Humphries was chatting sedately to two WAAF officers. The ensuing exchanges have all the period charm you would expect. 'Ladies were present', so modesty had to be preserved. Humphries pushed Goodale into one of the train lavatories and set off in search of the missing trousers. He explained:

> Either I succeeded in getting his trousers back, or I lost mine too. I
> hoped it wouldn't be the latter. I pushed my way into the carriage where

I knew the ceremony had taken place. The wicked gleams were still there. I sighed, hoping for the best. I could see Trevor-Roper there. [Flt Lt Richard Trevor-Roper, rear gunner in Gibson's crew] He would just love to remove my pants! I tried to be offhand.

'Excuse me chaps, have any of you by any chance seen Goodale's trousers?'

A roar of laughter greeted the question.

'Why, has he lost them Adj.?' questioned Dave Maltby innocently.

'You know he has,' I said. 'Now look chaps, I'm not trying to be funny, but he has just walked into a compartment and stood in front of a couple of ladies – like that!'

They roared at this until tears streamed down their faces. Jock Fort gasped,

'Quite well made, isn't he?'

Another shriek of laughter from all and sundry. I was getting nowhere.

'I think it's frightfully funny too,' I said, 'but you wouldn't think so if it happened to be your lady friends, now would you?'

The crisis had passed.

''No, come to think of it I wouldn't,' said Dave Maltby.

He pulled a pair of RAF blue trousers from underneath the seat. They were crumpled and covered in cigarette ash. Dave dusted them in a lazy sort of way and tossed them in my direction.

'Thanks,' I said, 'I'll make sure he puts them on.'

'Have a Scotch before you go Adj.' said Trevor-Roper, fumbling in a suitcase.

I didn't really feel like one but thought I had better accept. He handed me the top of a vacuum flask, half full of neat whisky.

'Go on shorty, let's see you knock that back,' he said.

I gulped, my prestige was at stake. Taking a deep breath I took the contents of the cup at one swallow. I nearly went through the roof of the carriage. My throat burned away at the sudden contact with the raw spirit, my head swam and tears came to my eyes as I gasped for breath.

''I'm proud of you Adj.,' said Trevor-Roper. 'Like another?'[63]

A version of this story also appears in Paul Brickhill's book. Debagging, putting footprints on the ceilings of messes, parading round dining tables with yard brushes on fire – this kind of behaviour was tolerated amongst officers on the grounds that they were undertaken by people

---

63 Humphries, *Living with Heroes*, p.46

who regularly put their lives at risk and were simply 'letting off steam'. It's a recurring theme in Brickhill's book, and also in R C Sherriff's script for the 1955 film. In the film, a fictitious incident of this kind gives the David Maltby character, played by George Baker, one of his dozen or so lines. Emerging from the riot caused by one throwaway remark too many from the anonymous officer from 57 Squadron, played by Gerald Harper (later to star in *Adam Adamant Lives!*) Maltby says to Gibson, 'Thank you sir. Saved my life. Never forget it.' Horseplay of course wasn't confined to officers. It was acceptable on occasions if conducted by other ranks, but there was always the undercurrent that it could be curtailed at any time by some chap with stripes on his arm.

Occasionally, when we were children, my mother would tell us about the times she used to visit David at various RAF bases during the war, and the pub sessions that inevitably accompanied them. She claimed that she was taught how to swallow a pint of beer in one go by some air force types, and once demonstrated this impressive skill to us with a pint glass full of water. But, as you get older, and your own late teenage years gradually fill with incidents you wouldn't necessarily want your parents to find out about, this kind of talk took on a slightly embarrassing quality. So it is with the older generation – families who go away on holiday and return to find their houses wrecked by 'friends' of their teenage children invariably describe their own offspring as 'quiet and well-behaved' and say that they could never have imagined them behaving in such a manner. It's as much of a shock for parents to find out that their children indulge in smoking, drinking and debagging as it is for the children themselves to discover that their aged parents still occasionally have sex.

The investiture took place the following day. There were plenty of hangovers amongst the 617 Squadron deputation but they all made it on to the palace on time. Tickets were available for parents and other relatives so Ettrick, Aileen and Jean were all present. Nina – heavily pregnant – does not seem to have gone. This was the second Maltby family outing to the palace in six months, since they had all travelled there in February 1943 (also staying at the Piccadilly) when David received his DFC.

To everyone's surprise, the investiture was conducted by the Queen, as the King was away in North Africa. The delegation from 617

No one seems sure who to follow as a large group of newly decorated 617 Squadron personnel march away outside Buckingham Palace. David Maltby is sixth from the left, John Fort is fourth from the right.

PHOTO: IWM/HU62924

squadron was first, headed by Wg Cdr G P Gibson, VC, DSO & bar, DFC & bar, now the most heavily decorated airman in the British empire. The 33 other officers and NCOs followed. Afterwards, photographers jostled and shouted as different groups were organised for pictures. Photos were taken of them all in a group, then the Canadians together, the Aussies together, then a bunch marching (badly) away.

After another drinking session, some of the group grabbed the chance to catch up on a few hours sleep before the party in the Hungaria Restaurant. It was in honour of 'The Damn Busters', as a famous misprint on the menu card states. In another error, the squadron is congratulated on 'their gallant effort on the Rhur Dams'. Besides the decorated aircrew, there were a number of other distinguished guests. Barnes Wallis was there of course, as well as Roy Chadwick and managing director Sir Roy Dobson from A V Roe, and from Vickers, Sir Charles Craven and Sir Hew Kilner. The famous aviation pioneer T O M Sopwith was also present, and made a speech

THIS BELONGS
TO H.R.HUMPHRIES
(I THINK THERE IS
NO ADJUTANT JUST
LIKE ME!) THE SHIT

"DAMN BUSTERS"

Dinner to celebrate

the decoration

of members of

617 Squadron R.A.F.

following their gallant effort
on the Ruhr Dams.

Given by A. V. ROE & Co Ltd.

TUESDAY, 22nd JUNE 1943.

THE HUNGARIA RESTAURANT
DORLAND HOUSE
14-16 REGENT STREET
LONDON · S·W·1

MENU

VINS

Coffee Cocktail

Cocktails

Crème Santé

Villanyi Rizling, 1929

Caneton Farci à l'Anglaise
Petits Pois à la Menthe
Pommes Nouvelles

Egri Burgundy Voros, 1930

Commendador Ports

Asperges Vertes, Sauce Hollandaise

Fraises au Marasquin

Menu card. David Maltby's signature appears twice on the back cover. John Fort's is on the inside.   PHOTO: LINCOLNSHIRE COUNTY COUNCIL, GRANTHAM MUSEUM before presenting Gibson with a silver model of a Lancaster aircraft. Gibson made a speech afterwards, managing to thank everyone involved, not forgetting the groundcrew, 'back room boys' and the workers at A V Roe. Then a picture of the breached Möhne Dam, brought by Barnes Wallis to the dinner, was given back to him, signed by most of the people who had taken part in the raid. He had the 'before' and 'after' pictures framed and hung them on his study wall, writing afterwards that they 'formed a historical record of this out-standing accomplishment on the part of the RAF.'[64]

The copy of the menu in the RAF Museum was donated to the Museum by the son of 'Monsewer' Eddie Gray, a popular comedian of the time who was an occasional member of the Crazy Gang. His nick-name derived from part of his stage routine where he spoke a mixed-up Cockney version of 'Franglais'. He was one of the entertainers who turned up at the end of the dinner and provided an impromptu cabaret – some of the others were Arthur Askey, Jack Hylton, Chesney Allen and Pat Taylor. Many of the menus were circulated for people to sign, and the one Eddie Gray took home has both David's and 'Johnnie' Fort's signatures. Gibson managed to sign it twice. Harry Humphries' copy, now in the Grantham Museum, has many of the same signatures and the cryptic comment on the front, 'This belongs to H.R. Humphries (I think there is no adjutant just like me) The shit'. It's not clear whether Humphries wrote this himself, or whether it is a contri-bution from one of his admiring colleagues. As there was copious amounts of free drink on offer – cocktails, a 1929 Rizling [sic], a 1930 Burgundy and Commendador port – there is a certain amount of con-fusion in the accounts of the night.

The food must have appeared impossibly exotic to people more accustomed to one sausage a week – crab cocktail, 'caneton farci' (stuffed duck) with 'pommes nouvelles', 'petit pois' and asparagus. My mother Jean, who had gone back that morning to her job cooking in a Leicestershire prep school, must have thought the menu pretty amaz-ing. It was a bit of a contrast with struggling to make the most out of the meagre ration allowances of a schoolful of small boys.

Some time late in the evening, a famous photograph was taken in which a number of people seem pretty worse for wear. Standing rather awkwardly at the back are a number of knighted bigwigs, alongside the newly promoted but always glum looking Air Cdre Whitworth, whose

64 Quoted in Sweetman, *Dambusters Raid*, p.247

Group photograph taken in the Hungaria Restaurant, 22 June 1943. Although the dinner was given by A V Roe, senior personnel from many of the other main aircraft manufacturers were also invited. A key to many of the people in the picture can be seen below.

PHOTO: LINCOLNSHIRE COUNTY COUNCIL, GRANTHAM MUSEUM

pyjamas had so famously formed the trophy at the party in the early morning after the raid itself. Most of the uniformed guest form an untidy group, sitting on the floor. Slap in the middle at the front, between Guy Gibson and Mick Martin, sits David, a huge distracted grin on his face. Behind him in line astern sit the other two crew members of AJ-J who were present, John Fort, a glass in his hand, and Vivian Nicholson. Round Vivian's shoulders can be seen an arm, with a hand holding a glass. It is that of Jack Leggo, the Australian navigator in Micky Martin's aircraft, who was the squadron's Navigation Leader. In Leggo's other hand there is a large cigar. Behind Vivian, with the smoothed-back fair hair, is Gibson's rear gunner and squadron debagger-in-chief, Richard Trevor-Roper. It's not a great photograph technically – a few people are obscured, some are looking sideways – but it freezes that moment in time when, in the words of Vivian Nicholson's mother a few months later, they were 'so young, happy and beautiful.'

The train back to Lincoln the next day was pretty quiet. It was probably a good thing that no training took place. However, on the Thursday, it started again and in the next ten days, David's crew undertook another six training exercises. Most of the time he was flying Lancaster EE130, a new aircraft that had arrived at the squadron to replace one lost at Chastise, and coded AJ-A. But on some flights he was back in AJ-J, J for Johnnie, and it was this aircraft that he was flying on Thursday 1 July, the day his son John was born. After a two hour flight (low-level cross country, high-level bombing at St Tudwells) he landed at Scampton at about 8.25pm and must have rushed off immediately. John Goodson Maltby was born at home, in Woodhall Spa, at 10.45pm – the 14th male in the Maltby direct line, as his grandfather Ettrick proudly recorded. I doubt that David was present in the room – husbands didn't do that kind of thing in those days – but we can picture the traditional scene, wearing out the carpet, waiting for the midwife to emerge with the good news.

The publicity machine was still making demands. During late June and early July, the well-known society and war artist, Cuthbert Orde was commissioned by *The Tatler* magazine to draw portraits of some of the 617 Squadron personnel involved in the Dams Raid. Those whose portraits appeared, in the issue of 1 September, were presumably selected as being the types who would appeal to readers of the magazine.

" Dam Busters ": By Cuthbert Orde

Some of the Men Who Destroyed the Ruhr Dams

Early in the morning of May 17th a force of Lancaster bombers led by W/Cdr. G. P. Gibson struck a devastating blow at the Ruhr industries, when they breached the walls of the great Möhne, Sorpe and Eder dams. W/Cdr. Gibson, who received the V.C. for this exploit, and several of the other members of the aircraft crews who participated in the operation, all of whom were decorated, appear on this page.

P/O. K. W. Brown, C.G.M.

P/O. W. C. Townsend, C.G.M., D.F.M.

Left: P/O. William Clifford Townsend, born at Sharpness, now lives at Cheyenne, Monmouthshire. Formerly in the Royal Artillery, he transferred to the R.A.F. in 1941, winning his decorations in May 1943, while a Flight Sergeant

Right: F/Lt. Harold Brownlow Martin was born in Sydney, Australia, in 1918, and educated at Lindfield College. He served first in the Australian military forces, transferring to the R.A.F.V.R. in 1940, winning the D.F.C. in 1941, and the D.S.O. in May this year

Below: S/Ldr. David John Harfield Maltby, born in 1920 at Hastings, Sussex, enlisted in the R.A.F.V.R. in 1940, and was commissioned a year later. He was awarded the D.F.C. in August 1942, and won a Flight Lieutenant when he won the D.S.O. for the Ruhr dam operation

P/O. Kenneth William Brown, born in 1920 at Moose Jaw, Saskatchewan, enlisted in 1941 in the R.C.A.F. He received his decoration for his part in the breaching of the Ruhr dams, at which time he was a Flight Sergeant

Below: W/Cdr. Guy Penrose Gibson, leader of the attack on the German dams, was born at Simla, India, and educated in England. Before transferring to Bomber Command he was a night-fighter pilot. He accompanied Mr. Churchill to Canada last month, to give him some of the R.A.F. the benefit of his flying experience

F/Lt. D. J. Shannon, D.S.O., D.F.C.

F/Lt. H. B. Martin, D.S.O., D.F.C.

F/Lt. David John Shannon is an Australian, and was born in 1922 at Bridgewater, South Australia. He enlisted in the R.A.F., and was trained in Canada, winning the D.F.C. in January 1943, and the D.S.O. in May this year

F/Lt. J. C. McCarthy, D.S.O., D.F.C.

S/Ldr. D. J. H. Maltby, D.S.O., D.F.C.

W/Cdr. G. P. Gibson, V.C., D.S.O., D.F.C.

F/Lt. R. D. Trevor-Roper, D.F.C., D.F.M.

F/Lt. Joseph Charles McCarthy comes from Long Island, U.S.A. He trained under the Joint Air Training Plan, and was commissioned in the R.C.A.F. in 1941. He won both his decorations in May 1943

F/Lt. Richard Dacre Trevor-Roper was born in 1915 at Shanklin, I.O.W. His home is in Nottingham. He was educated at Wellington and the Royal Military Academy, Woolwich, and served for some years in the Royal Artillery. In 1939 he enlisted in the R.A.F., being commissioned in 1941, and won the D.F.C. in November 1943

Double page spread from *The Tatler,* 1 September 1943, featuring Cuthbert Orde's drawings.   PHOTO: FAMILY COLLECTION

Gibson, of course, has the biggest picture on the double page spread. Besides David, there are also sketches of David Shannon, Joe McCarthy, Ken Brown, Bill Townsend, Mick Martin and Richard Trevor-Roper. The pictures appear to have been drawn on various dates in June and July, which suggests Orde paid more than one visit to Scampton. Orde drew hundreds of RAF portraits during the war, and some seem to me to be rather crudely executed. But the 617 Squadron portraits are sensitively drawn and amongst his best work.

Around the same time, an official RAF photographer took an extraordinary series of about a dozen colour transparencies, which are now held in the Imperial War Museum. Some show various crews, mainly of them sitting on the grass against a dark sky which looks as though a severe storm is brewing. Another is of Gibson sitting in a field of poppies, reading a copy of Morte D'Arthur (a bizarre choice of book,

David Maltby and Guy Gibson in the Squadron CO's office at RAF Scampton. Taken in July 1943, but exact date unknown.   PHOTO: IWM/TR1122

surely). And there is one of him with David, taken in the Squadron CO's office attached to Scampton's No.2 Hangar. Gibson has a pipe clenched between his teeth, and both men have a finger on the same page of some sort of picture book. Some sources have dated this as being taken on 22 July, but as David was in Blida in Algeria that day this can't be correct.

Exactly a fortnight after John was born, 617 Squadron was back on operations. Gibson was technically still in command of the squadron, but Sqn Ldr George Holden, who had previously commanded 102 Squadron in 4 Group, had been posted in and would shortly take charge. As he had previously flown Halifaxes, Holden had to become familiarised with flying Lancasters, but by Thursday 15 July he was ready to lead one team of five aircraft to Italy; David would lead the other. Gibson saw them off, watching from the marshalling point with Harry Humphries. For many of the crews who flew that day, it would be the last time they saw him.

The mission was to bomb two electricity transformer and switching stations, at Aquata Scrivia and San Polo d'Enza. Because these were beyond the 'out and back' flying range of the Lancaster it would be necessary to fly on to another airfield to refuel and reload. Blida, some 30 miles from Algiers, now in Allied hands after the victories in North Africa and used as a launch pad for operations in the Mediterranean, was the obvious choice.

Everyone was delighted with the chance of getting their knees brown, so they packed sunglasses and tropical kit and stowed their service issue suitcases and kitbags in the body of their aircraft. It was a long flight but largely without incident, and with very little opposition en route or over the target. David reported that he had bombed on target at San Polo d'Enza and seen blue flashes. One bomb and some incendiaries had 'hung up' but they had later successfully dropped these on the Genoa–Spezia railway line at Sestri Levante. He landed at 0745, having taken off from Scampton at 2215. Les Munro's aircraft was damaged by shrapnel from his own bomb casing – damaging the bomb aimer's panel and bursting his starboard tyre. This meant that his landing at Blida was dodgy, but he brought it down successfully.

Blida was fun at first. For many of the aircrew, including David, this was the first time they had set foot outside Britain. There was wine to drink, exotic fruit and food to enjoy, sunshine to bask in. Lots of photographs were taken, including the one of David's crew taken next to the aircraft which they used for this operation, AJ-A. This is the picture I saw for the first time when I started work on this book.

I now feel that I know the seven men in the picture better than when I first saw it more than a year before. Harold Simmonds' sister Grace Blackburn, from whose collection it came, doesn't know who took it or exactly how Harold got hold of it, but other copies must have been made, since one is also in the Nicholsons' family photograph album. It's a truism to say how young they all look, since apart from John Fort, they are all in their early 20s, but in one sense they also look quite old. It's the haircuts, the clothes, the gauntness, the greyness of the often-copied picture – I've noticed this before with shots taken during the war. These are men who seem already old before their time, and who will now never grow old 'as they that are left grow old'.

The weather closed in at Blida, which meant the 617 Squadron contingent had to stay for a total of nine days. People got bored, including the man lined up to take over as squadron commander, George Holden. According to Richard Morris, he was often regarded as weak and was prone to displays of arrogance. This was illustrated in Blida when he appalled other members of the squadron by gleefully driving a jeep straight into a flock of goats and goatherds.[65] We have no way of knowing how well he got on with David, at the time his fellow flight commander, but if David was anything like either of his sisters he would have found behaviour like that deplorable. Good manners, we were brought up to believe, were what defined you and that meant treating everyone you came across with civility and respect.

Eventually the crews got away and were instructed to bomb the docks at Leghorn (Livorno) on the way back to England. Again, it was a long flight, taking off from Blida at 2105 on Saturday 24 July, bombing at 0038 and landing at 0535 the next day. The bombing was uneventful, done on a time-and-distance run from Corsica, and everyone got home safely. The crews loaded up the aircraft with souvenirs, crates of fresh fruit and vegetables and bottles of Benedictine and wine. Mick Martin was wearing a red fez when Harry Humphries met him at the dispersal point.

Gibson was on the point of departure. He had been to lunch with Churchill at Chequers on the Saturday, where he was told that he would shortly be going to America under the auspices of the Ministry of Information. He finally left on Tuesday 3 August, after fitting in a trip to see one of the local women, a nurse, with whom he had been involved while his wife was in London.

Round about the same time that David and the rest of the Blida contingent landed at Scampton another 779 RAF bombers were also touching down at other bases all over England, following a massive attack on Hamburg. This was the first of four devastating attacks in the next ten days on the North German city. For the first time, the crews dropped 'Window' as they flew over enemy territory, strips of tinfoil designed to confuse the German radar, and it worked well. So well indeed, that on the night of the second attack on 27–28 July, a firestorm was created in the densely built up residential district of Hammerbrook when all the fires joined together and started sucking the oxygen out of the surrounding air. The firestorm lasted three hours and only subsided when all the burnable material in the area was con-

---

65 Morris, *Guy Gibson*, p.187

David as part of a tug of war team. The uniform and unsuitable shoes suggest that this was not an organised sports day

PHOTO: LINCOLNSHIRE COUNTY COUNCIL, GRANTHAM MUSEUM

sumed. It is estimated that 40,000 people died.[66] The name given by Bomber Command to the series of raids – Operation Gomorrah – with its connotation of a city being destroyed by the wrath of God was aptly chosen. Here was Harris's 'area bombing' strategy being used to its full potential.

Doubtless there was discussion in the Scampton messes between the 57 Squadron contingent, who participated in the Hamburg raids, and the 617 Squadron aircrew, who did not. There was certainly resentment that 617 Squadron was not being sent out on operations, a feeling that must have been intensified when on 29 July nine aircraft, including David's, were dispatched on a really soft trip. They went on a 'nickel run', dropping leaflets on cities in Northern Italy, and going on to Blida again. Seven of the nine flew back two days later, while Les Munro and Joe McCarthy had to hang about waiting for essential repairs.

Discussion in the mess was academic since it had been decided that 617 Squadron was not going to be used for run of the mill bombing operations, even on mass raids which needed hundreds of planes. They were to use Upkeep in further trials, and they were earmarked to

66 Middlebrook and Everitt, *Bomber Command War Diaries*, p.413

Official photograph of 617 Squadron aircrew., taken in July 1943, shortly before Gibson's departure. David Maltby's crew is identified with numbers: 1: David Maltby, 2: John Fort, 3: William Hatton, 4: Victor Hill, 5: Vivian Nicholson, 6: Harold Simmonds, 7: Antony Stone.

PHOTO: IWM/MH33960

try out the new 'thin cased' 12,000 lb High Capacity bomb which was nearly ready.

Gibson had been involved in meetings about the future of Upkeep right up to the moment of his departure, and had flown to a number of different locations both to assess the types of targets against which it might be used and to advise on defence mechanisms if the Germans succeeded in developing their own version. Air Ministry experts were now considering various canal embankments, some large dams in Italy and the Rothensee ship lift. With the invasion of continental Europe a possibility sometime in the future, changing the direction of spin on the mine to forwards and bouncing it against sea defences from the sea itself was another technique under consideration. Gibson

took David and squadron bombing leader Bob Hay to Shoebury Sands on 14 July to look at targets there.[67]

There was also the possibility of dropping Upkeep over land. This was tried in tests as early as 4 June when two 617 crews dropped forward spinning Upkeeps from 100 ft over the Ashley Walk bombing range in the New Forest. They bounced some 30–40 ft and travelled about a thousand yards but, unsurprisingly, peppered the aircraft with stones. Barnes Wallis watched these tests and said he was 'entirely satisfied' with the results.[68]

Screens and a concrete structure were now erected at Ashley Walk to provide targets and in August more tests were carried out there. Some of these tests involved landing at Boscombe Down, a few miles away. On one of these occasions, Antony Stone took the opportunity for a quick trip home to Winchester to see his family.

Fred Townsend was stationed at RAF Boscombe Down, and his wife Sibyl had been the next door neighbour of the Stones in Nuns Road, Winchester, when they were children. On this quick trip back to Winchester, Antony met up with Fred and because Fred was able to take him back to Boscombe the next morning Antony was able to stay

67 Morris, *Guy Gibson*, p.189
68 Sweetman, *Dambusters Raid*, p.258

overnight with his family. It was the last time they would see him.[69] This may have happened on the night of Wednesday 4 August, since the A Flight Authorisation Book shows that David landed at Boscombe Down in the afternoon. He flew back to base that night, but returned the next day. He seems to have had a full enough aircraft on this second trip as Air Commodore Whitworth and Plt Off Ken Brown were also on board.

John Maltby was baptised on 11 August by the Rt Rev Henry Skelton, a family friend who had been appointed the Bishop of Lincoln in 1942. The following day, 12 August, was Ettrick's 58th birthday: as he was a man who enjoyed country sports, it was always a source of amusement in the family that he had been born on the Glorious Twelfth, bang on time for the grouse shooting season. Ettrick and Aileen had come up from Witherdon and stayed at the Eagle Lodge Hotel at Woodhall Spa. After the christening, Aileen went on to Little Houghton and then Abersoch in North Wales, while Ettrick stayed on in Woodhall for a few more days. David was flying most of the time but on Monday 16 August, after a morning spent on low level-bombing practice, he called back to the house and saw his father. Ettrick recorded the event:

> 16 August: Saw David for last time (tho' did not know it). He came over from Scampton for a quick tea at Kenilworth. We just sat & talked & he just jumped up at about 5.30 & was going off with the usual 'so long cheerio' etc but instinctively I grasped his hand & he seemed pleased –

Of all the entries in Ettrick's diary this is one of the longest, and I wonder if it was the hardest for him to write. The heartfelt '& he seemed pleased –', the final long dash, an aching memory of a clasp of hands between a father and son who probably weren't used to showing emotion. They came from a generation that didn't even have the 'awkward manly hug' to fall back on. I imagine him: weeks, months later, working out exactly which date this 'quick tea' had occurred, turning to the diary, writing it in, wondering whether he had captured the moment aright.

It's a phenomenon not easily explained but the human brain seems to be hotwired to remember the last time we see a loved one before their death. There are countless accounts from wartime histories of

---

69 Correspondence, Fred Townsend to Alan Kinge, undated (1993?)

catching a glimpse of a son or daughter, a brother or sister, a father, mother, cousin waving from a train or unexpectedly turning at the corner of the street for a last look back. So great is their poignancy that each story has the ability to catch you in the throat as you read them.

Ettrick left Woodhall the next morning: luckily for him, as the Eagle Lodge Hotel was bombed that night:

17 August: I left Woodhall to go to Birkenhead to see Audrey and her [in] laws. The Eagle at Woodhall was bombed the same night – 10 hours after I'd left. Mrs Armour was rather badly injured. Lucky escape!

We can't be sure when the rest of the crew saw their families for the last time. For Vic Hill it was also probably some time in mid-August, since in a letter to his brother-in-law Don on 10 July he wrote that he was hoping to see his wife Eve again the following month:

I think everyone must know Eve & myself on Cardiff station now as I say cheerio to her there so often. Val made it even harder this time, when I left, she was standing on the door with mam, waving her little hand and saying 'Daddy' that gave me one thought, well this is certainly worth fighting for. I'm sure you will love her when you see her again Don I don't think Val was walking when you saw her last...
Well Don, roll along August 11th and lets hope we meet this time. [Spelling and punctuation as in original.][70]

For the rest of August, after he had seen Ettrick on the 16th, David flew just twice more from Scampton, once on another short training flight, and then on Monday 30 August to ferry groundcrew to the squadron's new base, at Coningsby.

---

70 Hill (Ashton) family correspondence, 10 July 1943

Chapter 9

Dortmund Ems

The squadron had to move from Scampton because its grass runways were to be concreted over. A return to Coningsby would have been very convenient for David. It was only a few miles from Woodhall Spa, so he could be at home with Nina and John for at least some of the time. They were still living in Woody and Bettie's house, Kenilworth. Woody and Bettie's son Richard, then a boy of eight, and a pupil at Hydneye, remembers that last summer well. David taught him how to long jump across the flower beds, he recalls. Although domestic life, staying with relatives and with a young baby in the house, must have had its own stresses and strains it was surely possible for them to catch a glimpse of what the future might hold for them as a family after the war. They discussed taking over the Goodson family fruit farm at Frognall, outside Wickhambreaux. As a boy and a teenager, David had always enjoyed working with his hands – he built a bridge at Witherdon in May 1940 while waiting for his call-up papers – and he regularly spent time in his holidays working on the Hatfeilds' farm at Hengrove. Moving to Kent and having his own farm would have suited him well.

The war, however, still had to be fought.

Many of those who took part in bombing hated the killing of other people but somehow detached themselves from it. Leonard Cheshire himself wrote at the end of the war, when he was an RAF observer seeing the destruction wrought by the atomic bomb over Nagasaki, that he wondered whether the loss of life had been worth it. David Maltby was a sensitive young man, and was sometimes troubled by the thought that he had brought death to so many. Scampton's Station Commander during the Dams Raid, Gp Capt Charles Whitworth, obviously knew this but it's difficult to see how he could have personally witnessed

David shooting at plates with a service revolver, to relieve the tension after an operation, which is the story he told George Baker on the set of the film, ten years after the war. David only served under his command at Scampton from March to August 1943, in which time he flew on just three operations. It is unlikely that the event occurred after the Dams Raid, and on only one of the two trips to North Italy did they return directly to Scampton. However, Whitworth could have been told the story by someone else who knew David, perhaps from his 97 Squadron days.

Trials with the Dams raid weapon Upkeep were put aside, and new 12,000 lb thin-cased bombs were delivered to Coningsby. 617 Squadron was to continue its role as a specialist low-level bombing unit and deliver this, the biggest bomb the RAF had yet carried, in an attempt to breach another German key industrial target, the Dortmund-Ems canal. This waterway stretches over 150 miles, linking the Ruhr valley to the sea. At Ladbergen, near Greven, just south of the junction with the Mittelland Canal, there is a raised section where aqueducts carry the canal over a river. This had long been a target which the RAF was keen on attacking, but so far had failed to breach. Now it had a new weapon, three times the size of the normal 4,000 lb 'cookie'. The plan was to drop these from very low height into the soft earth embankments of the raised waterways. A delayed fuse would give the Lancasters time to get away before the huge explosion.

The plan was drawn up in great detail by Air Cdre H V Satterly, the Senior Air Staff Officer at 5 Group, and the man who had drawn up the final orders for Operation Chastise. Over 60 years later, sitting in the National Archives, turning the yellowing foolscap sheets on which the orders are neatly typed, I marvelled at the precision skills needed.

The eight Lancasters detailed for the operation were to be accompanied by six Mosquitoes, specially brought in from 418 and 605 Squadrons. Their role was to deal with searchlights, flak and any fighter opposition met along the way or over the target. The force was to be divided into two sections of four Lancasters and three Mosquitoes each, with the force leader commanding the first section and the deputy force leader commanding the second. The two sections would fly out by separate routes, maintaining formation if possible, crossing the English coast at 1,500 ft and then dropping to 100 ft over the North Sea. The deputy force leader would arrive first, and mark the area with three special parachute beacons dropped on an exact grid reference. If they didn't work, incendiaries were to be used instead. When all the Lancasters had arrived at the target, they would come under the control of the force leader, who would attack first. They were expected to drop their bombs in turn at a precise point within 40 ft of the western bank of the canal. The bombing height was to be 150 ft above the ground, at a speed of 180 mph. Once a breach had been caused, the aircraft were to drop their remaining bombs on alternate banks of the canal 50 yards further north each time until all the bombs were used up. The bomb fuses gave a delay of between 26 and 90 seconds, which was supposed to leave sufficient time for aircraft to get clear. The force leader was therefore supposed to ensure that at least two minutes was left between each aircraft's attack.

The 12,000 lb bomb they were going to drop was designed to take advantage of the Lancaster's bomb-carrying capacity. As with the Dams Raid, the Lancasters had to be specially modified for the operation, this time with special larger bomb-bay doors, making the bay big enough to hold the enormous weapon. In this case, however, the mid-upper turret that had been removed for the Dams Raid was still available. Because the canal was known to be heavily defended, it was decided to carry a full-time front gunner on this trip, so an extra gunner was brought in for each aircraft to ensure that all three gun positions were filled.

The bomb had been made in three sections bolted together with a six-finned tail unit on the end. It was so big that it needed special bomb trolleys to move it from the store and took 35 minutes to be winched up into the Lancaster.

The six Mosquitoes arrived on 5 September. Nearly every day after that they practised on co-operation flights with the Lancasters, which were still being modified. When the modifications were complete the Lancasters were tested out and then used on low-level bombing tests at Wainfleet. On one of these trips, on 9 September, David Shannon flew the aircraft David Maltby had started using, JA981 with the identification code KC-J, with Bill Hatton, Antony Stone, Vic Hill and Harold Simmonds on board. Also along for the ride were two of the Mosquito crew members Sqn Ldr Gibb and Plt Off Mills. (This was a new aircraft, and had only arrived at 617 Squadron on 3 September. It had been built at A V Roe's subsidiary works at Chadderton, near Oldham. The identification letter prefix KC had been assigned to 617

Squadron for use on aircraft acquired after the move to Coningsby. Aircraft already on the squadron retained their AJ prefix.)

By now, the two Davids, Maltby and Shannon, were close friends. David Shannon had become engaged to Ann Fowler, a WAAF officer attached to 617 Squadron, and they were due to be married on Saturday 18 September. David Maltby was going to be best man. (The Shannon-Fowler romance is a recurring theme throughout Paul Brickhill's 1951 book *The Dam Busters,* with many references to Shannon's youth and the moustache he grew to try and make himself look older.) Shannon was a neat and methodical man, and his papers are stored in the archives of the Imperial War Museum, including photocopies of his logbooks from the war. As David Maltby was Shannon's flight commander his signature appears in his logbook at the end of every month's entries from May to August 1943.

The raid was important enough to be given its own code name, Operation Garlic, and was scheduled for Monday 14 September. That morning George Holden asked Harry Humphries to draw up the battle order. Holden was to lead the first section of four, with Les Knight, Ralf Allsebrook and Harold Wilson. David Maltby would lead the second group: David Shannon, Geoff Rice and Bill Divall. Three Mosquitoes would fly with each group. As deputy force leader, David Maltby was due to drop the special parachute beacons which would mark the target.

The weather was not good, but it was decided to take off anyway. A separate Mosquito designed for meteorological work had already been sent to the target area and was due to report back. If it found that the weather was bad over the canal, then they could call the strike force back.

There is no doubt that the crew knew how difficult this operation was going to be. They hadn't flown over Germany since the Dams Raid almost four months before and in the run-up to the operation and at the briefing it must have been obvious that they were being asked to take part in another raid which would demand the utmost levels of skill and crew co-operation. Once again, they were using a brand new weapon, never before dropped in anger and, once again, they would have to fly to their target and attack it at an almost suicidally low height.

But they were prepared. They were a team. The seven crew members that had flown together in AJ-J to the Möhne Dam and back had been together for nearly five months, flying for hundreds of hours, even though they had only completed four operations. They had flown together, eaten together, drunk together. They knew each other's habits, superstitions and foibles.

We can't be certain, but it's likely that Vic Hill stayed in his Dams Raid position of the front turret, while the extra gunner, Wt Off John Welch took the mid-upper position. (Welch had been posted to 617 Squadron in early August, after completing a tour of operations in 218 Squadron, and had a DFM to show for it. Like David, he had spent part of his between-tours posting on 1485 Target and Gunnery Flight instructing trainee gunners and bomb aimers.) The rest of them would have settled down in their normal positions: Harold Simmonds in his lonely turret at the rear of the aircraft, 40 ft away from the rest; Antony Stone, promoted to Flight Sergeant nine days earlier, by the radio set; Vivian Nicholson at his desk under the astrodome, with his charts and slide rules spread out; Bill Hatton on the right-hand side of the cockpit, hands clamped to the throttles, eyes constantly checking the instruments in front of him; John Fort probably stood behind him, unlikely to want to spend the first part of the trip lying down in the nose. In the left-hand seat sat Sqn Ldr David Maltby DSO DFC, veteran of 32 operations, commander of A Flight, father of one, sinker of pints, champion debagger.

There is a discrepancy in the documents about the time of take-off. One source says it was 2329, another 2340. They set course for their crossing point on the Dutch coast, south of Texel Island. Then came the news from the Mosquito on weather-spotting duty. The target was badly obscured by mist and fog. At 0038, a recall signal was sent from the operations room at 5 Group in Grantham. Just as, or just after, the recall signal was received, disaster struck and, somehow, David's Lancaster went down in the sea.

✳   ✳   ✳

It was while sitting in Cyril and Olga Nicholson's house, looking through an album with photographs of Vivian Nicholson's RAF career that I first heard of Len Cairns. Olga mentioned that Len had a long-standing interest in the fate of David Maltby's crew, and showed me some pages from the typescript of a book he was writing. When I got round to ringing him a few weeks later, he told me an astonishing story.

When I first started researching this book David's first cousin Mary Tapp, who was ten years old when he died, told me that Ettrick and Aileen had long believed that the cause of David's final accident was not an error made by him in turning the aircraft, or of hitting someone else's slipstream, but that his Lancaster had been struck by a Mosquito 'which shouldn't have been there'. Her own father, Aubrey Hatfeild, an RFC pilot in the first war, was adamant about this fact too. 'He was too careful a pilot to have made an elementary error,' he often told Mary as a child.

However there is no mention of any Mosquito in any published account of the crash. These all rely heavily on Paul Brickhill's account in *The Dam Busters,* those paragraphs I had read and reread, time and again, as a boy:

> They were an hour out, low over the North Sea, when the weather Mosquito found the target hidden under fog and radioed back. Group recalled the Lancasters and as the big aircraft turned for home weighed down by nearly 6 tons of bomb David Maltby seemed to hit someone's slipstream; a wing flicked down, the nose dipped and before Maltby could correct it the wing-tip had caught the water and the Lancaster cartwheeled, dug her nose in and vanished in spray. Shannon swung out of formation and circled the spot, sending out radio fixes and staying until an air sea rescue flying boat touched down beneath. They waited up at Coningsby till the flying boat radioed that it had found nothing but oil slicks.
>
> Maltby's wife lived near the airfield, and in the morning Holden went over to break the news, dreading it because it had been an ideally happy marriage. Maltby was only twenty-one. The girl met him at the door and guessed his news from his face.
>
> 'It was quick,' said Holden, who did not know it was his own last day on earth. 'He wouldn't have known a thing.'
>
> Too stunned to cry, the girl said, 'I think we both expected it. He's been waking up in the night lately shouting something about the bomb not coming off.'[71]

Brickhill doesn't quote any sources but we can guess that he must have

---

71 Paul Brickhill, *The Dam Busters,* Evans Brothers, 1951, pp.117-8

derived this account from talking to David Shannon, and perhaps also Brian Goodale, the wireless operator in his crew, who between them directed the air sea rescue launches to the site while Shannon circled above.

There are several inaccuracies in Brickhill's account: the air sea rescue service sent two launches, not a flying boat. One of the launches recovered a single body, David's. There was no trace of the rest of the crew. Brickhill was a journalist, not a historian, and as usual, he relies on accounts from eyewitnesses recalled several years later without looking at any primary sources. (To be fair to him, it should be pointed out that many of these sources were still classified under the 30 year rule, and therefore did not become available until the 1970s.)

Official documents and other contemporary accounts therefore tell a slightly different story, and have a number of significant variations. The most immediate account is probably that in Shannon's own logbook, which he would have written up almost straightaway. The entry reads in full:

> Operations – Dortmund Emms [sic] Canal. 1 x 12,000. 4 incends. (90x4). 2 marker beacons. Recalled weather u/s. Jettisoned. S/L Maltby crashed in sea. All killed. Directed Air Sea Rescue launches which arrived in about 1½ hours. Circled 3 hours in touch with 5 Group. Total flying time: 4.15[72]

It's a very bald account of the death of a close friend. Now he needed a new best man for his wedding, and it was only four days away.

The next official account was written in the 'operation summary' section of the 617 Squadron Operation Record Book. This would have been written by the Squadron Adjutant, Harry Humphries. It reads:

> … At approximately 0040 hrs, on the 15th, a recall message was sent to all aircraft, on account of unfavourable weather. The aircraft were then over the North Sea, and in turning to make the homeward journey the aircraft piloted by S/Ldr Maltby was seen to crash into the sea. Nothing definite is known of the cause of this accident, but it is possible that the aircraft struck the water. …[73]

Harry Humphries also wrote a more personal account in the notes he

---

72 David Shannon Logbook, photocopy held in Imperial War Museum archive
73 617 Squadron ORB, AIR 27/2128

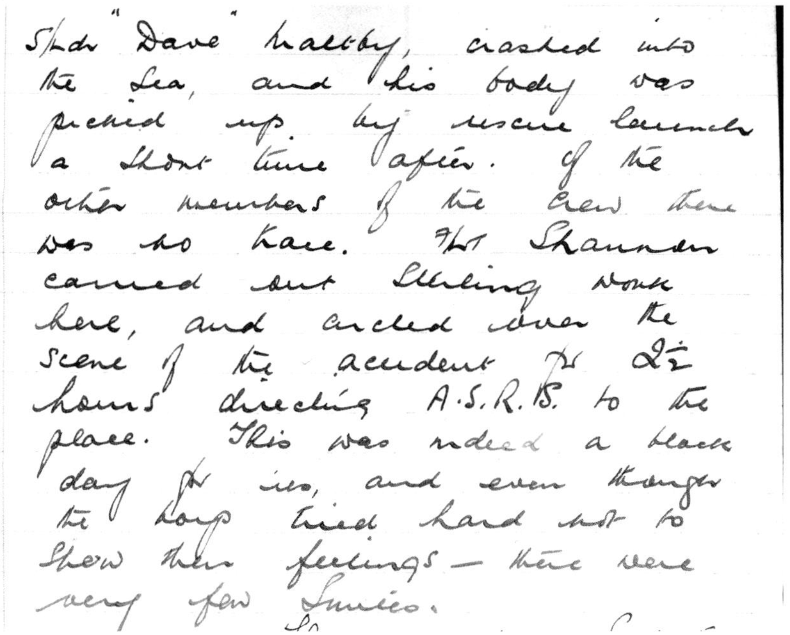

[Handwritten facsimile:]

> S/Ldr "Dave" Maltby, crashed into the sea, and his body was picked up by rescue launch a short time after. Of the other members of the crew there was no trace. F/Lt Shannon carried out sterling work here, and circled over the scene of the accident for 2½ hours directing A.S.R.B. to the place. This was indeed a black day for us, and even though the boys tried hard not to show their feelings — there were very few smiles.

Harry Humphries' handwritten account of the final accident.

was making for the story of the squadron that he planned to write after the war. There are twenty or more pages in a loose-leaf folder in Grantham Museum. They are not dated but are known to have been written in September 1943:

> Then came disaster of the first order. Our ever popular S/Ldr 'Dave' Maltby crashed into the sea, and his body was picked up by rescue launch a short time after. Of the other members of the crew there was no trace. F/Lt Shannon carried out sterling work here, and circled around over the scene of the accident for 2 1/2 hours directing A.S.R.B. to the place. This was indeed a black day for us, and even though the boys tried hard not to show their feelings – there were very few smiles.[74]

The accounts by Shannon and Humphries are the most important sources, since they are the most contemporary. Shannon's logbook entry is interesting for what it doesn't say. For instance, there is no mention of turning or catching another aircraft's slipstream. This

74 Harry Humphries MS notes in Grantham Museum

would suggest that he did not see the crash directly, but surmised it afterwards. How much would he have been able to see directly at night in poor weather conditions? Humphries knew both that rescue launches had arrived, and that one had recovered a body. However, in his 2003 book[75] he recalls that there was quite a lot of confusion on the night, and that 'garbled reports' circulated after the remaining Lancasters landed at Coningsby. '[S]ome wicked stroke of misfortune' caused the aircraft to hit the sea. What could the garbled reports have said?

There are also other official accounts. Every unit of the RAF, from a squadron upwards, has its own Operations Record Book, which means that an incident like this was recorded in other places. The first of these is the record book for 617 Squadron's station, RAF Coningsby. Its report differs slightly from the version found in the squadron's record:

> ... Owing to weather conditions, the formations were recalled at 0030 hrs. Shortly after receiving the recall, the majority of a/c observed a terrific explosion on the sea. This is presumed to be S/Ldr Maltby who failed to return.[76]

The slight variations in times are probably not too significant, but what is interesting is that the account is curiously vague about who, other than Shannon, 'observed' the explosion. A week or two later a formal Accident Card was prepared by a small panel, or perhaps even just one officer. The panel would have considered the information sent in by the squadron in writing and then summarised its findings:

> Time: 00.45. Ops night. Recall to base.
> A/c missing. Presumed hit sea. Investigators consider the accident was due to aircraft hitting the sea after some obscure explosion and fire had occurred in the aircraft. It is possible that the pilot partially lost control in a turn when the bomb doors were opened to jettison the bombs. Explosion and fire may have been caused by bouncing on the water. None of the equipment is likely to have exploded in the air.
> Cause obscure.
> Only e/a [enemy aircraft/action] could have set bombs or incendiaries on fire in the air. NB Large bomb doors affect aircraft stability when lowered.
> [Conditions] Night, moon, dark.[77]

75 Humphries, *Living with Heroes*, pp.65-66
76 RAF Coningsby ORB, AIR 28/171
77 Accident Record Card, RAF Museum

There is another mention in the RAF Coningsby ORB. At the end of each month, the medical officer would write an appendix detailing important medical 'events' which had occurred in that time. Although he does not appear to have been directly involved in the incident, he saw fit to include it amongst the accounts of bomb store accidents and football injuries:

> 14.9.43. One aircraft from 617 Squadron reported to have crashed in the sea – S/Ldr. Maltby and crew. Body of S/Ldr. Maltby was recovered from the sea and taken to R.A.F. Coltishall. Death was due to multiple injuries.[78]

These five accounts allow us to put together what we might call the 'official version', the one which has been repeated in slightly different versions in most of the reference books.[79] It goes like this:

After the recall, while turning, David's aircraft suddenly faltered and hit the sea. There might have been an explosion, caused when the incendiaries were jettisoned, or the 12,000 lb bomb might have shifted. It's unlikely that the big bomb went off accidentally: this would have caused a huge explosion and it is unlikely that any bodies would have been recovered. It was either an accident or mechanical failure or pilot error – but which of the three was never established. David's body was recovered, but the rest of the crew were presumed lost.

The truth may be different, for, as Len Cairns has discovered, there is a good chance that an errant Mosquito was involved. Most people have discounted this theory since the six Mosquitoes seconded to the mission from 418 and 605 Squadrons all returned safely. However another Mosquito on a completely different operation to attack Berlin did not come back. And Len Cairns is convinced that it was this one that collided with David's Lancaster.

The evidence for this is buried deep in the files held at the National Archives. The first clue is in the Operations Record Book for 278 Squadron.[80] This was the Coastal Command squadron which was responsible for air sea rescue on the Norfolk coastal area. Based at RAF Coltishall, about eight miles north west of Norwich, it flew Ansons for general searches and a Walrus flying boat for picking up ditched aircrew. The Air Sea Rescue launches from 24 ASR at Gorleston, which

---

78 RAF Coningsby ORB, AIR 28/171
79 But not all the standard reference books. Martin Middlebrook and Chris Everitt's account in their stunningly comprehensive *Bomber Command War Diaries*, p.430 wrongly states 'Maltby's body was washed ashore'.
80 278 Squadron ORB, AIR 27/1605

were directed to the crash by David Shannon's aircraft, were also administratively attached to RAF Coltishall. The 278 Squadron ORB records that an Anson was sent out the following morning from Coltishall to search. The full entry reads:

A/C ANSON No EG496

CREW
F/O SIMS, W F
F/Sgt HAMMOND, A
F/O DUNHILL, A
F/O RICHARDSON, K
W/O FRASER, R D

DUTY: Search position H.0374 for Lancaster and Mosquito reported to have COLLIDED.
TIME OF SEARCH: 06.38 – 07.56 hours.
Aircraft searched this position and found an oil patch approximately one mile long and 200 yards wide in which were small pieces of wreckage. Nothing further was seen and a 'FIX' was transmitted to operations after which A/C returned to base.

The squadron's entry is corroborated by a similar entry in RAF Coltishall's own Operations Record Book:

An Anson 278 Squadron was up 0638-0754 to search for wreckage of a Lancaster and a Mosquito which had collided during the night. A large oil patch one mile long and 200 yards wide was found approximately 53°05 N, 01°41 E, and though this was circled for 20 minutes, only small pieces of wreckage were seen. The Anson then returned to base in very bad weather.[81]

It's worth noting here that on 15 September 1943, with summer time still in operation, 0638 would have been not long after first light. The accident happened at about 0040, in the dark and in bad weather conditions. So at some time in the night, somebody in a senior position at Coltishall had been told that the accident was caused by a collision and had been requested to make a search at dawn.

81   RAF Coltishall ORB, AIR 28/168

Later that day a report had reached London. Every afternoon a group of senior officers would convene in a meeting room at the Air Ministry to discuss technical and administrative matters concerning Bomber Command. It was called the Air Officers Administration Conference (usually abbreviated in the files as the AOAs Conference). They would note details of the numbers of squadrons available, the ferrying of aircraft to and from different stations and the mechanical and other problems that had occurred. But they also looked at the numbers of operations flown, the losses incurred and, particularly, since they were interested in ironing out any repeated mechanical failures, which might be the cause of crashes. That very day, probably within 15 hours of the incident occurring, they noted that there had indeed been a crash the night before. The minutes of the conference state, quite baldly:

Crashed:
1 Lancaster of 617 Squadron and 1 Mosquito of 139 Squadron are believed to have collided N.E. of Cromer. No survivors yet reported.[82]

When Len Cairns read this extract out to me over the phone I could hardly believe it. 'You mean that the other aircraft can actually be identified?' I asked. 'Yes, it can', Len replied. It was one of a group of eight from 139 Squadron who had been despatched on a 'nuisance raid' over Berlin. One Mosquito, DZ598, had been recorded as 'did not return', as nothing had been heard from it after it took off from Wyton in Cambridgeshire at 1936 hours on 14 September. The pilot was Flt Lt M W Colledge and the navigator Flg Off G L Marshall.

The 139 Squadron records are, however, not very informative. The RAF Wyton ORB gives a little more detail about the raid:

This trip was made unusually difficult by heavy cumulonimbus, which caused several crews to return early and made the operation longer and more arduous for those who pressed on to the target.
F/L Colledge did not return; nothing was heard of him after take-off.
S/Ldr Braithwaite, F/O Mitchell and F/O Patient attacked Berlin in face of searchlights and moderate heavy flak.
S/Ldr Braithwaite received a Pasting from Brandenburg where he was coned for 10 minutes, and hit in eight places, though none serious.
Faced with the cumulonimbus, F/O Jackman attacked Emden and F/O

82 AOAs Conference, No 258, 15 September 1943, AIR 24/259

Swan attacked Borkum Aerodrome, by D.R. Technique, with unobserved results.

F/Sgt Wilmott and F/Sgt Marshallsay returned early having iced up in cloud and decided that they could not get through.[83]

The 139 Squadron ORB has a similar entry, with the added information about the weather in the North Sea: 'severe thunderstorms and heavy Cu-nim with some icing was encountered near the Dutch Coast'.[84]

There is no further information about what happened to Flt Lt Colledge's Mosquito. As nothing had been heard from him after take-off, and no wreckage was ever found, it has always been assumed that he was lost over the sea on the outward trip. Len Cairns' theory is that his radio failed, but he decided to press on to Berlin regardless. On the way home, his aircraft collided with David's.

It's certainly plausible. If Colledge had gone onto Berlin, he would have been coming back across the North Sea between 0030 and 0100, and his route from the northern end of Texel Island off the Dutch coast to landfall at Cromer would have intersected with the 617 Squadron Lancasters' route, which was due to take them from Coningsby to landfall on the Dutch coast just north of Petten. Plotted out on a map, the intersection point is very close to where we know the accident occurred.

Would Colledge have flown on to Berlin, even if his radio had failed? His background certainly suggests that he had the 'press on' attitude so beloved of senior RAF commanders. His full name was Maule William Colledge, and he was the elder of the two children of the distinguished throat surgeon Lionel Colledge. He had been in the RAF since the beginning of the war. He was known for his love of fast cars and flying, and once had a single seater plane at Brooklands aerodrome for his own use. His sister Cecilia also had an interesting career: she had been a champion figure skater since a very young age and had won a silver medal at the Winter Olympics, held in Lake Placid, USA, in 1936. She still lives in the USA, and remains a trustee of the Fellowship set up by the Royal College of Surgeons to promote and advance head and neck surgery in memory of her father. Little is known about the Mosquito's other crew member, its navigator, Flg Off Geoffrey Marshall, who was 30 and came from Brighton.

So we have three separate statements that there was a collision

83 RAF Wyton Station ORB, AIR 27/960
84 139 Squadron ORB, AIR 28/963

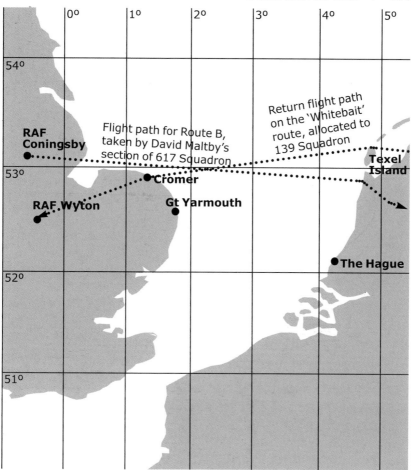

Map showing the routes allocated to the Lancasters and their Mosquito escort of 617 Squadron and the separate Mosquitoes of 139 Squadron, on the night of 14-15 September 1943. The 617 Squadron detachment was divided into two sections, with David Maltby leading the group taking Route B. This was to take them directly from Coningsby to landfall on the Dutch coast a little way south of Texel Island. The 139 Squadron Mosquitoes were following the 'Whitebait' route, the return leg of which runs from the northern end of Texel island to landfall at Cromer. The two routes intersect very near to where David Maltby's Lancaster crashed into the sea.

MAP DRAWN BY AUTHOR

between a Lancaster and a Mosquito, one of which mentions the squadrons involved. Another piece of evidence would surely be that of the ORB for the Air Sea Rescue unit which operated the launches. Maddeningly, this doesn't appear to have been preserved. At the time, responsibility for Air Sea Rescue was in the process of being passed from the navy to the RAF, and all the RAF records start just a couple of weeks later, on 1 October 1943. There are very detailed records for individual search and rescue operations from that date – but none from before.

This makes it very difficult to work out how information about a possible collision reached the Air Ministry and, indeed, what made someone there cite the squadron numbers at the AOAs Conference. Did they have some other evidence or, because there had been a report of a collision between a Mosquito and a Lancaster, and only one of each type had been lost on the night, did someone just assume that these were the aircraft and squadrons involved?

It should be said that the collision theory can only be supposition. There is absolutely no evidence that Colledge got as far as Berlin, and then decided to fly back at low level. If he did, without a working radio, he would have put himself in danger of being mistaken for a Luftwaffe intruder and being shot down. The 'collision' entries are from documents written up immediately after the incident, and may have arisen because reports of both a missing Lancaster and a missing Mosquito were misunderstood as a collision between the two by the dispatchers of the Anson search aircraft. It is even possible that the person who compiled the official Accident Card knew about this theory and discounted it when he wrote up the card a few days later.

Supposition it may be, but what is clear is that no one at 617 Squadron knew anything about a Mosquito being involved. Neither Shannon nor anyone from his crew (all of whom are now dead) ever said anything of the kind to John Sweetman, Robert Owen or others they spoke to over the years. However, they would not have denied, as Harry Humphries noted in his account, that there was a certain amount of confusion on the day. Also, it was dark and the weather conditions were poor. How much could they actually see? Nor was there much chance for further reflection on the circumstances of David's crash because the squadron suffered an even bigger disaster in the next 24 hours. The seven crews that returned safely to Coningsby in the early hours of 15 September flew back to the Dortmund Ems canal that night, with Mick Martin taking David's place. In very bad weather conditions they failed to damage the canal, and five aircraft were lost. Four complete crews and Les Knight, pilot of the fifth plane, were killed. (Knight's crew, including Fred Sutherland, still alive and well in Canada, baled out while Knight struggled to keep his damaged aircraft aloft. They all owe their lives to him.) George Holden, the squadron's new CO, was one of the men lost that day, and in his crew were four of the men who had flown with Guy Gibson on the Dams Raid. It would be understandable that in these terrible circumstances that no one sought to find out more about David's crash, and relied on what they had been told.

There are some other mysteries about the night of 14/15 September. The RAF Coltishall account states that David's body was recovered and taken to RAF Coltishall. If this was the case, then Coltishall's Medical Officer should have recorded this in his monthly appendix to his station's ORB, since he was responsible for the station's mortuary. Like his counterpart at Coningsby, the MO was a fairly assiduous record keeper. His September 1943 report contains accounts of a number of other incidents on the station, but there is nothing about David. In fact it is likely that David's body might never have reached Coltishall. According to Tony Overill, whose father served in 24 Air Sea Rescue, and who has himself written a history of the Unit, *Crash Boats of Gorleston,* bodies recovered at sea were taken to the civilian mortuary at Great Yarmouth, which was close to the harbour. He thinks that it would be very unlikely that it would then have been taken from there to Coltishall.

Also, it is not clear exactly how David died. The MO at Coningsby states that the cause of death was 'multiple injuries'. This would have been likely if there had been some sort of explosion on board. However, David's widow Nina told her daughter Sue, many years later, that when she saw his body there was only a small bruise on his forehead, and no other obvious marks at all. This suggested to her that he had been knocked unconscious, and died from drowning.

As we have seen, and it is confirmed by Humphries, George Holden called over to see Nina in Woodhall Spa on the morning of Wednesday 15 September, to tell her what had happened. Paul Brickhill's account of their conversation (see p.153), where he doesn't even give her a name, may not be accurate, because it is difficult to see how he sourced it. It was, as he says pointedly, Holden's own 'last day on earth'.

By the afternoon, Ettrick and Aileen, down in Devon, knew and must have set about telling the rest of the family. As in all bereavements, routine work acts as displacement from the act of grieving. Funeral arrangements have to be made, letters written, notices placed in the newspapers. It's impossible to know how much of this was done by Nina and her parents, and how much by Ettrick and Aileen.

As for the families of David's crew, the first news they got was by telegram. That day brought the dreaded knock on the door to seven households up and down the country, from Sherburn to Burgess Hill, from Winchester to Wakefield. In each case, the news must have been made worse by the knowledge, slowly gleaned, that their sons were 'missing', with no bodies yet recovered. There would be no need for funerals for them.

To the Stone family in Winchester, the loss of Antony was such a severe shock that his mother, Mrs Dorothy Stone, set off by train for Woodhall Spa to find out more. She was shown into Harry Humphries' office in a state of shock, disarming him by saying that she was glad that there were brave men like him left to carry on the fight. As he wrote afterwards, the only battles he fought were against official letters and forms.

David's body was brought to Wickhambreaux for burial. On the Friday, Ettrick and Aileen had driven up from Devon to Hemel Hempstead, where they would stay the night with Aileen's sister Violet and her husband Ted. It's a 200 mile trip that nowadays, with all the motorways, you could do reasonably in under four hours, but at that time must have taken them seven or eight hours in their Buick. I remember that road well from my childhood holidays in Cornwall. In the 1940s, and indeed through to the early 1970s, you drove through, not round, most towns and villages: Okehampton, Honiton, Ilminster, Ilchester, Mere and Wylye, their very names almost needing to be pronounced with a West Country burr. On those holidays, in the late 50s and early 60s, I would sit in the seat behind my father, leaning forward over his shoulder to note the number of miles we had driven every hour, working out the average speed, predicting what time we would get our first glance of the sea somewhere near Bodmin. For Ettrick and

Notices in *The Times* and a Kent local paper.

Aileen, going the other way, the journey must have been interminable. What do you say to each other, driving across Salisbury Plain to your son's funeral?

A notice appeared in the Births, Marriages and Deaths column of The Times on the morning of Saturday 18 September. Throughout the war this had a special section for those killed 'on active service'. The funeral, it announced, was to take place 'to-day (Saturday) at 2.30'.

The following week the Kent newspapers gave full accounts of the funeral, emphasising David's local connections. The *Isle of Thanet Gazette* wrote:

One of the heroes of the great 'dam-busting' operation at Moehne and Eder, Squadron-Leader David John Hatfeild Maltby, D.S.O., D.F.C., a grandson of the late Captain C.T. Hatfeild of Hartsdown, Margate, and of the late Mrs. Hatfeild, who was Mayor of Margate, has been killed on active service, with 'all his gallant crew'.

Two other papers listed the mourners. Nina's name does not appear in either, so perhaps she chose not to go. Aileen and Ettrick had come from Devon, Audrey and Johnnie from Birkenhead, Jean from... I don't know where – aged 18, she was just about to start a new job as the caterer at Merchant Taylors' School in Northwood. George and Hilda Goodson, and Bettie and Woody Walter represented the Goodsons. All of these were almost outnumbered by Aileen's family, the Hatfeilds, with three of her brothers, Herbert, Aubrey and John, her sister Violet and their spouses all in attendance. Flg Off Lance Howard, who had been the navigator in Bill Townsend's Dams Raid crew and who appears in the Hungaria Restaurant picture, represented 617 Squadron. The service was conducted by the Rector, Rev W E Daniels, and Mr C Wells played the organ. We are even informed of the hymns that were sung, led by the choir, including the stirring Vaughan Williams tune, 'For All the Saints'.

A few days later there was an obituary in *The Times*. It was described as being written by 'a friend', so we have no way of knowing who actually wrote it, but because the writer makes reference to David when he was a little boy I wonder if it might have been his uncle, Aubrey Hatfeild. Although these obituaries were common enough in wartime editions of *The Times* there is a genuine generosity of spirit in the tribute:

> One cannot praise too highly the great courage, steadfastness of purpose and leadership that David consistently displayed during the two and a half years he was with Bomber Command, especially when one remembers the exceedingly shy little boy, diffident of his own capabilities. He was, even to those of us who knew him well, unwilling to talk of himself, let alone his achievements, and always gave the credit to others. This was so apparent after the famous raid on the Moehne Dam, for which he was awarded the D.S.O. According to him, every bit of its success was entirely due to his very fine crew, his grand ground staff and magnificent Lancaster.[85]

---

85 *The Times*, September 1943

The piece goes on to praise David's 'modesty and unselfishness which endeared him to all but also his deep sense of humour and joy in the really simple things of life.' These are much the same sort of sentiments expressed by Harry Humphries, who wrote a series of moving short pen portraits about the officers he knew, who had been killed on both 14 and 15 September. These are in the same file in Grantham Museum as the description of the loss of David from which I quoted on p.155. Humphries had joined the RAF at the beginning of the war. He desperately wanted to fly, but he failed the medical and was forced to take an administrative job. However he never lost the flying bug and became very close friends with many aircrew. He felt their loss very deeply, and his accounts make sad reading. There are entries about both David and John Fort:

DAM BUSTER S/Ldr Maltby DSO DFC Killed 14/9/43
This huge good-natured pilot had a natural aptitude for being popular. He just could not help himself and was hero worshipped by his crew. Flying to him was a thing of joy and an opportunity to release his high spirits. This was often emphasised by his 'take offs' from the dispersals, and his love of low-level flying. In the mess he was always like a big schoolboy, always ready for a practical joke. A good pilot, a good officer, a good friend, above all a good man.

...

DAM BUSTER P/O J. Fort D.F.C. Air Bomber S/L Maltby's crew
A Lancastrian with an outlook on life difficult to beat. Good humoured, slow of speech, but quick in action. A small fair-haired chap, with broad shoulders, well able to carry their responsibilities. He had been in the Service for some years and often said it was a "piece of cake" compared with the competition & throat cutting of civilian business. A very popular member of the Squadron.[86]

It's a bit of a cliché to say that war changes lives, but in many cases, and certainly in David's, it is true. If there hadn't been a war, he might have finished training as a mining engineer. (Did Ettrick think he might help him find a job in South Africa, where he had a brother and other family?) Or he might have gone into farming, which was obviously something towards which he had a leaning, even if he hadn't met and married Nina. However, barely out of his teens, he discovered that he

84 Humphries, MS Notes in Grantham Museum

It would perhaps be a good thing to write a few lines on the skipper and personalities missing on this raid.

DAM BUSTER S/LDR Maltby DSO DFC Killed 14/9/43

This huge good natured pilot had a natural aptitude for being popular. He just could not keep himself, and was hero worshipped by his crew. Flying to him was a thing of joy, and an opportunity to release his high spirits. This was often emphasised by his "take offs" from the dispersals, and his love of low level flying. In the mess he was always like a big schoolboy, always ready for a practical joke. A good pilot, a good officer, a good friend, above all a good man.

DAM BUSTER. P/O J. Fort DFC in Bomber S/L Maltbys crew.

A Lancastrian with an outlook on life difficult to beat. Good humoured, slow of speech, but quick in action. A small fairhaired chap, with broad shoulders, well able to carry their responsibilities. He had been in the Service for some years, and often said it was "a piece of cake" compared with the competition & throat cutting of civilian business. A very popular member of the Squadron.

Harry Humphries' affectionate pen portraits of David Maltby and John Fort.

PHOTO: LINCOLNSHIRE COUNTY COUNCIL, GRANTHAM MUSEUM

had an aptitude not only for the extremely difficult job of flying a heavy bomber but also for leading a team under fire. Then, because of a combination of circumstances and luck – surviving one tour and coming back on operational duty at the right time – he was selected for the raid which became the most famous operation ever undertaken by the RAF ('our Waterloo or Trafalgar' according to one historian to whom I was chatting one day, while researching this book). But his luck, and that of John Fort, Bill Hatton, Vic Hill, Vivian Nicholson, Harold Simmonds, Antony Stone and John Welch, ran out over the North Sea, shortly before one o'clock in the morning of 15 September 1943.

Chapter 10

*

Aftermath

The two attempts to bomb the Dortmund Ems canal were the final proof that low-level bombing by Lancasters was far too costly in terms of numbers of crews lost. Throughout the whole war the RAF only flew two such operations. Both of these were undertaken by 617 Squadron, and only one of these was a success. The crew loss statistics speak for themselves: although two targets were destroyed on the Dams Raid, eight out of nineteen crews had been lost. A staggering six out of nine aircraft were lost on the two days that the squadron set out on its failed mission to the Dortmund Ems canal. This makes a total of 14 out of 28: an attrition rate of exactly 50 per cent. It's unlikely that any RAF squadron in the whole war had such a level of losses over two consecutive operations (which to all intents and purposes they were – the sorties over Italy in July 1943 were only stopgap affairs). No. 617 Squadron had many more successes later in the war, but it never flew at low level again.

Some time after the accident, Ettrick must have decided to write up his diary to include David's operations. In the last quarter of 1943 he recorded very little new information: the only three entries for October show Aileen going to Wickhambreaux on 6 October, Miss K (presumably, Miss Kennedy, a teacher) having her appendix removed on 21 October, and the arrival of Audrey, Nina and the two grandchildren, Anthea and John, at Witherdon on 26 October. In November 1943 he noted little more than Jean was taken ill with pneumonia and went into hospital soon after starting her new job catering at Merchant Taylors' School. December brought little more cheer, although Nina came for Christmas, with the six-month-old John and her parents, George and Hilda. Audrey, her nine-month old daughter Anthea, and Jean were also there. The year which had seen the birth of Ettrick and Aileen's first two grandchildren had been hit by tragedy.

It's impossible to be certain but I guess that at either the October or Christmas visit, Nina brought David's logbook and Ettrick decided to copy out all the information he didn't have. This would explain the arrows in his entries placing 1941 and 1942 dates above those from 1943. Perhaps he also wrote up the other entries about David's last visit and the last tea in Woodhall Spa at that time.

At some point in this period he wrote to some, if not all, of the relatives of the rest of David's crew. The letters he sent have been lost, but I have a copy of the reply from Mrs Elizabeth Nicholson, mother of Sgt Vivian Nicholson, and an extract from a letter left for his parents by Sgt Antony Stone. These have both been typed, but not by the original writers. When I showed a copy of the letter written by his mother to Vivian's brother, Cyril Nicholson, he was adamant that his mother could not type and would have written any letter by hand. The fact that the extract from Antony Stone's letter is typed on the second sheet of paper would indicate that it was typed by the same person, probably Ettrick himself. Certainly he could type – he owned a small portable typewriter which we had in the family for many years after he died.

Mrs Nicholson's letter is heartbreakingly eloquent both in her expression of her own grief and her feeling for someone else suffering in the same way:

Dear Mr Maltby

I scarce know how to write this letter, but I hope you will forgive my husband for not answering your kind and sympathetic letter to us, for which we thank you most sincerely.

My husband has been trying ever since to find time to write, but owing to have to work so much overtime in essential work, up to now has found it impossible so I am trying to write instead.

I am the mother of your son's navigator Flt/Sgt Vivian Nicholson D.F.M. and my husband and I send you our deepest sympathy in the great loss you have sustained. We got an awful shock when we received a telegram saying our son was missing on the night of 14/15th Sept.

Then a letter four days later saying he was missing on a training flight after their plane crashed over the sea and despite extensive air/sea rescues operations, only the body of the Captain was found with very little hope for the survival of the rest of the crew.

80 Front Street
Sherburn
Durham

Dear Mr Maltby,

I scarce know how to write this letter, but I hope you will forgive my husband for not answering your very kind and sympathetic letter to us, for which we thank you most sincerely.

My husband has been trying ever since to find time to write, but owing to having to work so much overtime in essential work up to now has found it impossible so I am trying to write instead.

I am the mother of your son's navigator Flt/Sgt Vivian Nicholson.D.F.M. and my husband and I send you our deepest sympathy in the great loss you have sustained. We got an awful shock when we received a telegram saying our son was missing on the night of the 14/15th Sept.

Then a letter four days later saying he was missing on a training flight after their plane had crashed over ???????? the sea and despite extensive air/sea rescueoperations, only the body of the Captain was foun with very little hope for the survival of the rest of the crew.

Then two days ago we got another letter saying they were on operatio against the enemyand not on a training flight. They had to tell us about the training flight for security reasons.

We would like to know the true facts of how and what they did that night and would be gratefully thankful if there is any news you would kindly give us.

We knew from our son they were a proud and happy crew, and we have at least four different photos of your gallant son, his bomb aimer and our boy together with others taken while in London June 22/23rd.

It is indeed a terrible and deep wound for us when we look at them s young,happy and beautiful.

We also knew as from what my boy told others, that, they knew the daily risks they had to run, but were prepared to face them as it was for a good cause, which surely makes us feel all the more proud of them, although our loss is at times unbearable.

Our boy was very conscientious, very guarded and painstaking in his speech telling us very little about his work or duties. We feel, for him to navigate to your gallant sons rank and to be in the 617 Squadron he must of had good capabilities. Please if your son ever told you anything to his credit, we would indeed be thankful to you if you would kindly let us know. In a letter from his Commanding Officer he said.

Vivian achieved excellent results in all his duties, his biggest job was when he navigated Sqd Leader Maltby to the German Dams in May. He was an Ace navigator the Air Force could ill afford to lose. This makes us feel there is something we would like to know.

Could you tell us, if your son was in command of the Squadron that night and if so would our son be leading navigator and have you the addresse of the rest of the crew, may we beg your kindness again by sending them to us, as we would like to write to their relations.

Please forgive mistakes and this long letter, but I know you will understand my yearning for any news, and I have the worry of our second so aged 19 on the Submarine H.M.Seanymph, which until Saturday when we receive a telegram saying he was now sharing the pain at the news of Vivian, we had'nt heard from him for seven weeks.

You have indeed one consolation in having the body of your gallant son.

This world owes so much to these gallant young lives and we feel that they are so greatly needed for the future. We can only wait patiently till we can understand why they are taken from our homes, where their places can never be filled.

Again,please accept our sympathy as we can fully understand what the shock and the blank are.

Yours very sincerely
Mrs A.T.R.Nicholson

P.S.
Please could you tell us if it was our boys crew who actually burst the Mohne Dam.

Extract from *letter left by*
Air Gunner Wireless Operator
Antony Stone to his parents.

"I will have ended happily, so have no fears of how I ended as I have the finest crowd of fellows with me, and if Skipper goes I will be glad to go with him. He has so much to lose far more responsibilities than I and you can rest assured and know that I've taken hundreds with me who lived as you do and never even gloried in the war as I did and I still experience that same thrill every time I fly"

Letter sent by Mrs Elizabeth Nicholson to the Maltby family, and letter left for his parents by Antony Stone, both probably typed by Ettrick Maltby.

Then two days ago we got another letter saying they were on operations against the enemy and not on a training flight. They had to tell us about the training flight for security reasons.

We would like to know the true facts of how and what they did that night and would be gratefully thankful if there is any news you would kindly give us.

We knew from our son they were a proud and happy crew, and we have at least four different photos of your gallant son, his bomb aimer and our boy together with others taken while in London June 22/23rd.

It is indeed a terrible and deep wound for us when we look at them so young, happy and beautiful.

We also knew, as from what my boy told others, that, they knew the daily risks they had to run, but were prepared to face them as it was for a good cause, which surely makes us feel all the more proud of them, although our loss is at times unbearable.

Our boy was very conscientious, very guarded and painstaking in his speech, telling us very little about his work or duties. We feel, for him to navigate to your gallant sons rank and to be in the 617 Squadron he must of had good capabilities. Please if your son ever told you anything to his credit, we would indeed be thankful to you if you would kindly let us know. In a letter from his Commanding Officer he said.

Vivian achieved excellent results in all his duties, his biggest job was when he navigated Sqd Leader Maltby to the German Dams in May. He was an Ace navigator the Air Force could ill afford to lose. This makes us feel there is something we would like to know.

Could you tell us, if your son was in command of the Squadron that night and if so would our son be leading navigator and have you the addresses of the rest of the crew, may we beg your kindness again by sending them to us, as we would like to write to their relations.

Please forgive mistakes and this long letter, but I know you will understand my yearning for any news, and I have the worry of our second son aged 19 on the Submarine H.M.Seanymph, which until Saturday when we received a telegram saying he was now sharing the pain at the news of Vivian, we had'nt heard from him for seven weeks.

You have indeed one consolation in having the body of your gallant son. This world owes so much to these gallant young lives and we feel that they are so greatly needed for the future. We can only wait patiently till we can understand why they are taken from our homes, where their places can never be filled.

Again, please accept our sympathy as we can fully understand what the shock and the blank are.

Yours very sincerely

Mrs A.T.R. Nicholson

P.S. Please could you tell us if it was our boys crew who actually burst the Mohne Dam.

The extract typed by Ettrick from the letter left by Antony Stone is much shorter:

"I will have ended happily, so have no fears of how I ended as I have the finest crowd of fellows with me, and if Skipper goes I will be glad to go with him. He has so much more to lose and more responsibilities than I and you can rest assured and know that I've taken hundreds with me who lived as you do and never even gloried in the war as I did and I still experience that same thrill every time I fly"

(In both letters spelling, punctuation etc as in original typescript)

Why did Ettrick type up these letters? Perhaps he wanted to make copies for the other families, or for the rest of his, and as there was no such thing as a photocopier in your local newsagent in those days, this was the easiest way. Whatever the reason, this is the only part of the correspondence that has survived.

How Antony Stone's letter reached Ettrick is not certain. It would seem likely that his family sent it to Ettrick, perhaps after he had written to them. Antony's mother, Mrs Dorothy Stone, had obviously found the news very hard to bear. Having travelled to Coningsby in an attempt to find out further details, she then sought out Antony's fiancée, Peggy Henstridge, and asked her to give back her engagement ring and photos of Antony. From a distance of over 60 years this seems rather a heartless thing to do, but, no doubt she had a reason.

One of Peggy Henstridge's nursing colleagues, Mary Clavey (née Rawlinson), remembered the day that Peggy had been told the news of Antony's death, in a letter to Alan Kinge in the 1990s:

I was doing nursing training at the Royal Hants County Hospital, as was Mr Stone's fiancée Nurse Henstridge... We were making beds together when she was called to the office to be given the sad news, after which she returned to the aforementioned task, and having told me very quietly what had happened, carried on making the same bed. The man in the bed could not help noticing her sad expression, and said to her 'You are looking very sad, nurse'. I nodded to him, and he said no more, obviously realizing that there was a very personal sadness. That was the way of life in the early 40s.[87]

Peggy Henstridge later married, becoming Peggy Gardner, and moved to Fareham. She became active in local politics, was elected to the council several times, and was Fareham's first ever Mayor, when it was upgraded from an urban district council to a borough in 1974. She was awarded an OBE for a lifetime's work in public service, and died in 2000. But she obviously never forgot her first fiancée, and Alan Kinge recalled to me how emotional she became when they talked about him a few years before she died. She told Alan that she had never seen Dorothy Stone again after the ring incident, but that she had remained in touch with Antony's father, Joe.

Mrs Nicholson's letter raises an interesting point about the circumstances of the crash. She says that they received two letters some time apart. In the first they were told that the plane had 'crashed over the sea' while on a training flight. Only when they received the second letter did they find out that the crew had been on operations, 'for security reasons'. Is it possible that whoever wrote the letter (usually it would have been the squadron commander, George Holden, but he was also dead) knew that a collision was being investigated?

It seems unlikely that Ettrick wrote about a collision with a Mosquito in his letter to Mrs Nicholson. If he had, she would surely have mentioned it in her reply, in the long list of questions about which she was seeking further information. But it would seem that, at some point, someone must have told Ettrick about the possibility and he told his brother-in-law Aubrey. Or, perhaps, Aubrey found out himself. He might have contacted senior RAF officers who he knew from his own First World War RFC days. His daughter Mary can't be certain exactly when her father told her that he knew the collision had been caused by a Mosquito 'which shouldn't have been there' but she is positive that it was soon after the crash.

The war went on inexorably throughout the autumn and winter of

---

87 Correspondence, Mrs Mary Clavey to Alan Kinge, 18 May 1993

1943-44. Even though a symbolic turning point in the war had been achieved with the invasion of mainland continental Europe in the toe of Italy in early September, fierce defence by German forces after the Italian government surrendered meant that the conquest of Germany from that route would be unlikely to succeed. On the Eastern front, the Germans had retreated to the Dnieper river but crossing that would be a huge challenge for the Soviet forces. An attack from the west was the only other alternative, and had long been planned for some time in 1944. Exactly when it would occur was still to be decided, and was of course a closely guarded secret. Meanwhile, in the air, Bomber Command was flying more and more missions over Germany, but still suffering severe losses. At Christmas 1943, many people must have reflected that Churchill's statement a year previously that the Allies had reached the 'beginning of the end' was more than a little optimistic.

It was obvious that a huge price was going to have to be paid to conquer Nazi Germany. Every landing undertaken, every mile moved towards Berlin, whether from south, west or east, was going to cost thousands of lives. Three of those, all army officers, would be David's cousins; Ettrick and Aileen's nephews.

Lt Charles Bartlet, the son of Aileen's sister Mildred and her husband Willy Bartlet, was almost exactly the same age as his cousin David. They had been boyhood friends, the two families sharing many camping holidays together. Although Charles had got into Cambridge, he left when he was called-up and joined the Worcestershire Regiment. He later transferred into the Irish Guards. After landing at Anzio in early February 1944 he was involved in one of the many intense battles with German forces and he was officially listed as 'missing'. He had married a woman called Mary Wilson on 1 June 1943 and she put Charles's name in the newspaper lists of servicemen missing in action, in the faint hope that she might get further information that way. More than 60 years later, Charles's sister Frances Bonsey still remembers how her mother Mildred was irritated by this. 'I wish she wouldn't do this, he's not coming back,' she would say. Charles's body was recovered later, and he is buried in the Beach Head War Cemetery in Anzio. The official date of his death is now given as 8 February 1944.

Capt Ralph Maltby was the son of Ettrick's older brother Francis and his wife Enid, and was also Ettrick's godson. Born on 3 October 1917, he was a little bit older than David and Charles Bartlet. He and his brothers Patrick and Roger had all been at school at Hydneye in the 1920s. He went on to Wellington, and then joined the Royal Artillery two years before the war started. He had been in France when it capitulated in 1940, and escaped through St Nazaire. In 1942, as an expert in anti-aircraft fire, he had been one of 16 officers who volunteered to fly as air gunners in bomber crews over Germany, in order to study German anti-aircraft defences at first hand. He was mentioned in dispatches and received an Order of the Patriotic War from the Soviet Union for this work. On 17 September 1944, three months after D-Day, he was an Intelligence Officer attached to the 2nd wing of the Glider Pilot Regiment, part of the 1st Airborne Division which landed by parachute and glider near Arnhem in the Netherlands. The German forces counter-attacked very strongly, and the Allied forces were driven back, sustaining hundreds of casualties. Ralph was killed by a shell in the cockpit of the glider in which he was flying as co-pilot, shortly before it landed, and he is now buried in Osterbeek War Cemetery. Ralph had one more thing in common with his cousin David – a young child. He had married Jean Beath in 1943, and they had a daughter, Rosamond, born early in 1944.

A couple of months later Lt Louis Maltby was also killed, serving in the South African Kimberley Regiment, part of the force driving up through Italy. He was the oldest of the three, born in 1914, the second son of another Charles, the youngest of the Maltby brothers. Always known by his family nickname 'Noonie', he had been in the army since the beginning of the war, and served in both the East African and North African campaigns. In November 1944, in fighting near Padua, in northern Italy, he was badly wounded and captured. He is officially listed as dying of wounds on 13 November 1944, while a prisoner of war, although his mother, back in South Africa, didn't find out about his death until April 1945.

In the early part of 1945, Ettrick and Aileen were told that they could begin to plan to go back to Hydneye. On 6 February, Ettrick was able to write to all the parents about this, and on 9 March the military finally 'relinquished' the building. By the end of March they were all back in Baldslow, but with a lot of work to do. They finally slept their first night in the house on 4 April, 'a very disturbed night', Ettrick recorded but gives no reason why this should be so.

The war was nearly over. On 1 May, he wrote fervently 'The end of

Hitler – Hound of Hell', and the next day recorded the good news that not only had all the German forces in Italy surrendered, but also Berlin had been captured by the Russians. A week later came the final surrender, and with it on 8 May, VE Day. Hydneye House School reopened for business that day, back in its own building, with 40 boys turning up for the summer term.

But for Ettrick and Aileen things were never going to be the same. They would have to learn to live, in the words of Carrie Kipling, a mother who had lost her only son in the First War, in 'a world to be remade without a son'.[88]

---

88 Tonie and Valmai Holt, *My Boy Jack,* Pen & Sword 1998, p. 166

Chapter 11

∗

After the war

B oth during and after the war, it suited the RAF to keep alive the memory of a one-off operation which combined an audacious method of attack, technically brilliant flying and visually spectacular results. These alone would have guaranteed the Dams Raid a secure place in history long after the war, but without the books, published in the 1940s and 50s, and particularly the 1955 film it would never have reached its current status as a cultural icon. The Dams Raid has become one of those events, beloved of journalists and TV documentary list-makers, which are supposed to epitomise Britishness. A good example is a typical rant by Daily Mail columnist Richard Littlejohn, in this case about a guide to UK citizenship issued by the Home Office. After 500 words of 'you couldn't make it up' fulmination he then pulls together an alphabetical list of 'what it means to me to be British':

> A is for Agincourt.
> B is for Bond, James; Bader, Douglas; Botham, Ian; bloodymindedness and Brylcreem.
> C is for Churchill, The Cruel Sea, Carry On; Connolly, Billy; Calzaghe, Joe; cricket and Chicken Tikka Massala.
> D is for the Daily Mail, Dunkirk, Dambusters and Dad's Army.
> E is for Ever Decreasing Circles, Edinburgh Castle, Ealing Comedies, Everton v Liverpool.[89]

And so on, and so on. You can guarantee that a 'rentahack' article like this will surface somewhere every few months, but what really gets the commentators (and nowadays the bloggers) going is some news peg specific to the Dams Raid. An anniversary, the auction sale of an artefact, or the subject that has exercised so many people over the last few

89 *Daily Mail,* 16 November 2007

years – the possible remake of the 1955 film. Who is going to star in it? Will it be Americanised? And, above all, will the dog's name be changed?

The process of giving the Dams Raid its special status had in fact started well before the end of the war. It began with the RAF's own public relations staff, who were assiduous in promoting the activities of Bomber Command in the media (for instance, BBC journalist Richard Dimbleby flew on no fewer than 19 operations).[90] Even before the raid took place, they had been aware of what tremendous propaganda it might make, and an official photographer was at Scampton both before and after the raid. The careful collection of press cuttings, starting the day after the raid, which I discussed earlier on p.121, is another indication of how seriously the PR staff took the job.

Throughout the summer and autumn of 1943 the official public relations initiative went on. The visit by the King and Queen to Scampton and the investiture at Buckingham Palace were both carefully choreographed, with copious details and several photocall opportunities being made available to the press. Harry Humphries remembers there being a PR person on the train from Grantham to London. This meant that the deaths of David and his crew on 15 September 1943, and those of the other Dams Raid survivors on the following day, were much more widely covered than that of other bomber crews lost around the same time.

Guy Gibson was in Canada at the time of the ill-fated Dortmund Ems raids, on the lecture tour and recruiting drive that would fast turn him into what Richard Morris calls a 'professional hero'.[91] In Calgary, he had met Mrs Hilda Taerum, the mother of his Dams Raid navigator Flt Lt 'Terry' Taerum and signed the scrapbook in which she was keeping all the memorabilia her son had been sending her. Three days later, Terry Taerum was killed, along with all the rest of George Holden's crew. It was front page news in the Canadian papers: 'Calgary's Dam Buster is reported missing'[92] read one local report.

A few weeks later, Gibson was in Hollywood, where he spent a fortnight as the guest of film director Howard Hawks. Ostensibly he was resting after his whirlwind passage through Canada and on to the USA, but it is likely that he also discussed Hawks's already expressed desire to make a film about the Dams Raid. According to Richard

90 Bishop, *Bomber Boys*, 2007, p.147
91 Morris, *Guy Gibson*, 1995, p.198
92 www.lancastermuseum.ca

Morris, Hawks had started work on this project only two months after the raid, in July 1943, and had recruited the young assistant air attaché at the British Embassy in Washington, a certain Flt Lt Roald Dahl, to write a script. Hawks was 'building a scale model of the Möhne Dam 300 feet long together with models of Lancasters 9 ft long powered by engines which will actually fly', wrote Dahl's boss, Sqn Ldr Allen Morris.[93]

Dahl appears to have completed at least one draft of a script, although unfortunately it does not seem to have survived. It was sent to Barnes Wallis who apparently condemned it as absurd, and the project was scrapped. Howard Hawks must also have lost interest, as by then he was probably working on his next film, *To Have and Have Not*, on which, of course, Lauren Bacall first met Humphrey Bogart. But the seed for a film project had been sown.

Richard Morris suggests that Dahl and Gibson collaborated on other projects, notably an article for the American magazine *Atlantic Monthly* called 'Cracking the German Dams'. This was later republished in the *Sunday Express* in Britain, without Gibson's consent, where it was retitled 'How We Smashed the German Dams'. Both versions of the article bore Gibson's name, but he certainly did not write it, and may not even have checked it as it contained a number of inaccuracies. The actual author may well have been Dahl. A lot of the material was later transposed straight into the manuscript for *Enemy Coast Ahead*, with some of the mistakes still included. Gibson did not even know that the article had been reprinted in a British newspaper, and had to undergo a certain amount of ribbing from Mick Martin and David Shannon when he met them again on his return from North America. The response from the public, however, was very positive and it was one of the factors that led to the next suggestion from the upper echelons of the Air Ministry and the Ministry of Information. Gibson was seconded to the Ministry, ostensibly to a desk job concerned with accident prevention, but in reality to write an account of his life in the RAF.

Writing this account, which came to be called *Enemy Coast Ahead*, took Gibson most of the first few months of 1944, which was also to be the last year of his life. He was given an office and, it would seem, a Dictaphone and access to typing facilities, since the original manuscript contains a number of mishearings and transliteration mistakes

---

93 Morris, *Guy Gibson*, 1995, p.207

(some of which survived right through to the finished book). When he finished the draft, it was circulated first to the official censors and then to an editor at its publisher, Michael Joseph. Both of these made a number of changes, the first to preserve various official secrets and the dignity of some senior service personnel and the second excising a number of Gibson's more reactionary statements and extreme views.

By the middle of September 1944, Gibson had finished checking through the revisions, and had written his comments in a number of notes which he then pinned to the original manuscript. (The entire object can be seen intact at the RAF Museum.) At the same time his long campaign to be allowed back on flying duties was beginning to bear fruit – with disastrous consequences. He had flown four operations between July and September 1944 when, on 19 September, he took off in a Mosquito to mark the bombing target for a force of Lancasters. Then at about 2230, mission accomplished, he died on his return flight, crashing near the small Dutch town of Steenbergen.

The crash was very severe, a fire ensued, and only parts of his body and that of his navigator, Sqn Ldr James Warwick, were ever recovered. The two were only officially listed as missing at the end of November. A few days later, on 4 December 1944, the *Sunday Express* printed the first instalment of its serialisation of part of *Enemy Coast Ahead* (for the *Sunday Express*, the war never seemed to end. It was still running real-life action stories as a double page feature until at least the 1970s, always accompanied by a large pen and ink illustration.).

Although the war was drawing to a close, there seems to have been no rush to get the complete book out. Michael Joseph's editors worked on the text throughout January 1945, making further minor revisions, and the final version went back to the censors at the Ministry of Information in February. It was returned by the end of the month.

Finally, in January 1946, it was published. It was a huge success, and the first impression sold out quickly. Amongst those buying it was my mother, who wrote her name in the copy I still have: *M Jean Maltby, Feb. 7th 1946.*

When I started writing this book, I took this copy down from the shelf for the first time in years. I have spent years working in book design and production and my first instincts on opening any book are always a subconscious appraisal of the production details, and then to see if they are confirmed on the title page verso. Typeset in Monotype Baskerville, I think to myself, cheap paper very typical of post-war economic standards, the only photographic illustration a tipped-in portrait frontispiece, cheap blue cloth-binding blocked in silver foil on the spine. As I turn to the imprint details, I'm glad to see that my type-spotting abilities are still intact. The book was indeed set in Baskerville, and printed by the well known book printers Unwins. First published in 1946, it says at the top of the page, and nothing else, meaning that this is a first edition. However, any intrinsic value it may hold is reduced by the fact that it is a very battered copy, the cloth has some slight tears, it is faded and bears a number of stains.

The book falls open at the beginning of the section on Gibson's days in 617 Squadron, which actually only occupy the last fifth of the book. These were the parts that we read as children, and I am sure that it would have been the first bit my mother would have sought out. At the top of page 242 is David's first mention. At the impromptu party on their first night in the mess, that I now know is heavily fictionalised, he is described as 'large and thoughtful; a fine pilot.'

After 18 months working on this book, I'm also now much more conscious of the errors which occur throughout *Enemy Coast Ahead*. Many of these survived the copy-editing and proof-reading supposedly done by Michael Joseph. Just on the few pages which cover the first days at Scampton, there are several misspellings of names – Foxley, Hevron and Humphrey for Foxlee, Heveron and Humphries, to name a few. But that is to detract from the book's qualities. Gibson had many faults, and was not a natural writer, but it has a candour and freshness which could probably only have been supplied by someone who did so much in the four or five years it covers. It is a book of its time, displaying all the certainties and much of the politics of someone who saw himself as a natural officer and leader. (Strange how he grew into that role. The CO of 5 Group, Sir Ralph Cochrane, told Max Hastings after the war that Gibson 'was the kind of boy who would have been head prefect in any school,'[94] but, in fact, Gibson's time at St Edward's was pretty undistinguished, and far from being head boy he never got above the middling rank of house prefect.)

Gibson's book ensured that the Dams Raid had a secure place in history but it would surely have faded slowly to the same level as some other audacious one-off operations, such as the midget submarine

94 Hastings, *Bomber Command*, p.216

attacks on the *Tirpitz*, if it hadn't been for the determination of the same Sir Ralph Cochrane. By 1950, he had become the second most senior officer in the RAF, the Vice Chief of the Air Staff, and it seems that it was he who was most determined to preserve the history of 617 Squadron, and its first operation, the Dams Raid. To do this, he brought in a professional writer, Paul Brickhill.

Brickhill had been a journalist in his native Australia before the war. Then he joined the RAAF and served as a fighter pilot both in Britain and the Middle East. He became a prisoner of war in 1943 after being shot down in Tunisia, and was held in the infamous Stalag Luft III, where he became one of the escape organisers. He was involved in planning what became called the 'Great Escape', although he did not take part in it because, apparently, he suffered from claustrophobia. After the war, he had gone back into journalism, but when a book he co-authored in 1946 with Conrad Norton, *Escape to Danger,* was a success he decided to try full-time writing.

Concentrating at first on his own experience, he wrote a full length account of the Great Escape in a book of that name, which was published in 1950. This too was a big success and brought him to Cochrane's attention. It would seem that Cochrane spoke to several others, including Leonard Cheshire and Mick Martin, before offering Brickhill the job.

By June 1950 Brickhill had started his research. He set out what he was planning to write about in a letter to Harry Humphries. What he wanted was 'human details, anecdotes, little sidelights':

> With the warm support of Air Chief Marshal Sir Ralph Cochrane I am preparing to write the history of 617 squadron, and he, Micky Martin, and others have given me your name as a man who knows most of the gen.
>
> It is not to be a formal history, but more of the human story of the squadron. Sir Ralph is very keen that it should be a story of the RAF spirit, and I quite agree.

At first, Humphries was extremely annoyed by this approach. When the squadron had first been formed, he replied, Gibson had asked him to keep notes with a view to some day writing its story. He had com-

piled over 100 pages of typescript, along with a host of other information. This put Cochrane and Brickhill in a difficult position, and they
had to wheel out Leonard Cheshire, who wrote to Humphries 'in the
name of the Squadron and with the purpose of ensuring that the history shall be as full as possible.' Humphries obviously idolised Cheshire
and he quickly agreed to co-operate.[95]

With Humphries on board Brickhill set out about the task quickly,
and then spent a lot of time interviewing Martin, Barnes Wallis and
others, supposedly in a hotel in Kensington.

For children like me, growing up in the 1950s, Brickhill's three best-
selling books *(The Great Escape, The Dam Busters* and *Reach for the Sky)*
and the films that followed came to define what we knew of the war, or
at least the part that had involved the RAF. Each had the same kind of
heroes, young officers, usually British but with a large dash of
Commonwealth input, struggling to achieve an unlikely victory not
only against the Germans but in the latter two also against a certain
sort of obstructive stuffiness in the upper reaches of Whitehall. They
are pacey, gripping narratives, peppered with dialogue which sounds
authentic, but must have been largely recreated by the author himself,
since he often puts it into the mouths of people long dead. As an
Australian, he didn't need any prompting to pay due respect to the men
from the Commonwealth who added a breath of irreverence to the proceedings.

He was very keen on a certain type of Britishness, what he called in
the introduction to *The Dam Busters* 'the British synthesis of talents'
where 'exceptional skills or ingenuity can give one man or one unit the
effectiveness of ten'.[96] This is a point that has been well expressed by
John Ramsden in his British Film Industry(BFI) monograph on the
Dam Busters film. In all Brickhill's books:

> ... success follow[s] refusal to give way to disappointment or defeat; a
> moral closely related to the national myth of Dunkirk, the Blitz and the
> Battle of Britain in 1940-41, but restaged as an inherent national trait by
> Brickhill in the individual war narratives of his books.[97]

In *The Dam Busters,* this characteristic is not only personified in the airmen but also in the person whom he obviously sees as the story's other

---

95 Humphries, *Living with Heroes,* p.107
96 Brickhill, *Dam Busters,* p.11
97 John Ramsden, *The Dam Busters,* Tauris, 2003, p. 20

true hero, Barnes Wallis. The first three chapters are almost exclusively about Wallis, and his struggles to design and then build a weapon which could attack massive structures like a dam. Brickhill's gift for explaining the complex engineering principles involved is sometimes overlooked by commentators who probably found it hard to get an O level in physics, but he displays a knack for boiling down the theory into a few sentences, and enlivening his narrative with little human touches:

> [Wallis] was aware that bombs and shells often buried themselves 3 or 4 ft in the ground before exploding, but that was so shallow the explosion forced its way easily to the top, causing a small crater, and the shock waves dissipated into the air. It was less effective than a surface explosion because the blast and shock waves went straight up instead of outwards.
>
> But if you could lock the explosion underground so it could not break out you would get a sort of seismic disturbance ... an earthquake! An earthquake bomb!
>
> The idea shaped in his mind while he was sitting in a deep chair in his home in Effingham, an unspectacular setting for the birth of something so powerful.[98]

Brickhill's account of Wallis is of course conflated in the public mind with his sympathetic portrayal by Michael Redgrave in the film, whereas he was, as has been pointed out since by a number of people, a rather more complex and difficult man. But the lonely genius up against the Whitehall bureaucrats is how Brickhill chose to paint him, and this is how he is now remembered.

The book was published in 1951, and was another instant success. The copy we had in our house when I was a boy was the Pan paperback edition, but now I have my grandfather's copy, also a first edition with Ettrick's initials EGM pencilled inside the cover. Book production standards had been relaxed by the time it was published, and it is a much more handsome object than *Enemy Coast Ahead*, set in a large size of Monotype Plantin. It is illustrated with a number of photographs, including the shot taken at the Hungaria restaurant on the night of the Buckingham Palace investiture. Brickhill (or perhaps a production assistant at Evans Brothers) has provided a number key to the individu-

---

98 Brickhill, *Dam Busters*, p.20

als gathered in a disorderly heap. This key, which I have seen repeated without attribution or alteration in other books, contains a number of mistakes, including wrongly identifying John Fort as Vivian Nicholson.

This cheerful scene is the only picture of David in the book, although he is mentioned a number of times in the text. Brickhill liked stories where 'the boys' let off steam, and he repeats many of those told to him. The debagging of Brian Goodale on the train to London, obviously derived from Harry Humphries, was obviously one that caught his eye.

In the early 1950s Associated British Pictures Corporation was the largest of the British film production companies, owning Elstree studios, Pathé News and other parts of the industry. Soon after Brickhill's book came out ABPC's Director of Production, Robert Clark, bought the film rights for £7,500, giving Brickhill half and allocating the rest for a screenwriter.[99] Clark was looking for a vehicle for one of the studio's contract stars, Richard Todd, but whether he had noticed the physical resemblance of Todd to Gibson is not certain. Fairly soon afterwards he recruited Michael Anderson as director, Michael Redgrave to play Wallis (another close resemblance) and, crucially, R C Sherriff to write the script.

Anyone like me who went to an all-boys school in the 1940s, 50s or 60s would straightaway know Sherriff's name, because in 1928 he wrote the play *Journey's End* which, with its all male cast of a dozen or so, was a perfect vehicle for school or house plays. It is the story of a group of First World War infantry officers and the pressures they were under in the trenches before a major attack near the end of the war.

What Sherriff captured beautifully in *Journey's End* was the way in which British officers of the period spoke. In fact he could almost be said to have invented the genre of film in which laconic understated dialogue is the order of the day, since after the play's success he had spent a number of years in Hollywood. Recruited by Sam Goldwyn as a scriptwriter and editor just at the time, in the early 1930s, that 'talkies' were taking off, he wrote films like *The Invisible Man*, *Goodbye Mr Chips* and *The Four Feathers*. He even worked as an unaccredited script editor, on one of the doyens of the genre, the wartime weepie *Mrs Miniver*. Although set in England, this film was actually produced in Hollywood and must have needed the touch of a real-life Brit on the script.

---

99 I owe these details and much of this chapter to John Ramsden's very useful (and entertaining) book in the British Film Guide series, *The Dam Busters*, Tauris, 2003.

Although Sherriff hardly mentioned the script for *The Dam Busters* in his own autobiography it is now widely acknowledged as one of his best pieces of work. His style, updated with RAF slang and ways of speaking from the Second World War, has many touches which show that a master craftsman was at work. For instance, there is a great line given to Wallis, confronted by a bureaucrat telling him how difficult it would be to get him use of a Wellington bomber for test drops. 'What possible argument could I put forward to get you a Wellington?' Wallis replies, 'Well, if you told them I designed it, do you think that might help?' In the next scene, we see the Wellington in the air.

For once, ABPC allowed the production budget for *The Dam Busters* to go above the £150,000 they normally set as a maximum, which allowed them to use real Lancasters, and real RAF crew to fly them, for the aviation sequences. They could only get four aircraft, so they had different numbers painted on each side to allow them to look like more. (Real aviation buffs can tell that the Lancasters used in the film were made after the war, by the types of guns in the rear turret and the absence of engine exhaust manifolds.)

Extra verisimilitude was added by cutting in the real sequences shot during the war of the bombing test runs, a decision made easier by the use of black and white film and a traditional screen-ratio. Michael Anderson, the director, was a great admirer of the wartime British documentary film movement, which had featured the work of people like John Grierson and Humphrey Jennings, and wanted to incorporate this look in *The Dam Busters*.

When it came to the casting, it wasn't just Richard Todd and George Baker who were given roles because they bore a similarity to their off-screen counterparts. This led to difficulties for some of the actors, such as the very British Nigel Stock (later cast as Dr Watson in the 1970s *Sherlock Holmes* TV series) playing the Australian 'Spam' Spafford. His attempts to talk Strine were often mocked by the real Aussies such as Bill Kerr, who was cast as Mick Martin.

Much of the film was shot at Scampton, using some of the real locations, with the flying sequences taking place both there and at the nearby RAF Hemswell. There was a certain amount of confusion during filming between real RAF personnel and actors, with numerous tales of actors getting salutes to which they weren't entitled, and complaints that actors playing NCOs were allowed to eat in the officers' mess.

Still from *The Dam Busters*. The set for the briefing room scenes in the film was an accurate reproduction of the original at Scampton. George Baker, playing David Maltby, at the back of the group towers over the shorter actors playing the other pilots.   PHOTO: BFI

The film's final ingredient, its music, has added so much to its place in history that it's almost a surprise to find out that it was only added after shooting was finished, although this is standard practice in the movie business. What is a genuine surprise to most people is to find that Eric Coates's work was not completely original. He reworked a march he had written during the war as a tribute to the victors of El Alamein to make the famous theme. Additionally, a pedant or quiz buff will tell you that it is not correct to say that Coates 'wrote the music for the film'. The only part of the score, the most famous bit of course, that was written by him is the Dam Busters March – the film itself was scored by the well-known film composer Leighton Lucas.

When the film was finished there was so much interest that it had two Royal Premieres, on consecutive nights, 16 and 17 May 1955, to coincide with the twelfth anniversary of the raid. Princess Margaret went to the first, the Duke and Duchess of Gloucester to the second. The way in which these were conducted can be seen as contributing greatly to the mixing of fact and fiction. Surviving members of 617 Squadron, next of kin of those who died, Barnes Wallis and his family and wartime and post-war leaders of the RAF mixed with the cast and crew from the film, with musical accompaniment from the RAF Central Band and a march past by the Air Training Corps band. There was even a model of the Möhne Dam, alongside which Barnes Wallis and Richard Todd posed for pictures.

It seems odd now, but there was then a four month gap before the film went on general release. However this gave ample time for cinemas around the country to stoke up publicity, and they did not fail. Once again, they were encouraged to get the RAF involved in local premieres. ABPC produced a 'publicity book', giving local addresses and phone numbers for RAF Associations (for veterans) and local 'area publicists' in RAF regional offices. Cinemas were encouraged to get an RAF band to play on the opening night and even to let the service have a recruiting stall in the foyer. Cinemas were also encouraged to invite local relatives of those who had died on or after the Dams Raid. For the local premiere in Newcastle, one cinema sent a chauffeur-driven car the 30 miles to Sherburn in Durham to collect Vivian Nicholson's mother, Mrs Elizabeth Nicholson.

In fact the publicity was hardly necessary since *The Dam Busters* proved to be a big success at the box office. Even though it had only opened in September, it was the top-grossing film of 1955 in Britain, taking over half a million pounds at the box office, thus already making a profit for ABPC within a few months of its release.

When it was released internationally it was also a hit in the Commonwealth, particularly in countries which had provided crews for the original 617 Squadron. The use of real Australian actors like Bill Kerr probably helped here. But it did not do very well in the USA, much to the annoyance of Richard Todd, who thought that ABPC wasn't putting enough muscle behind it. He arranged a private showing for some of his Hollywood friends including the producer Darryl F Zanuck who is reputed to have said: 'Gee. That's one hell of a picture. Is that a true story?' When Todd replied 'Absolutely' (English understatement again!) Zanuck asked 'Then why doesn't it say so?'[100]

Zanuck had a point, of course. No one in Britain needed to be told

---

100 Ramsden, *Dam Busters*, p.115

Life at Hydneye in the 1950s. Christening party for George Foster, with Ettrick Maltby trying to organise a group photograph. Photo taken by John Blackburn. The author and his cousin, David Blackburn, both aged 2, are in the front row examining their shoes.   PHOTO: FAMILY COLLECTION

that it was a true story. It was a familiar enough tale to the average cin-emagoer only twelve years after the actual raid. Familiar it may have been but most people would not have known enough of the detail to spot the fictionalisations introduced by the artistry of Sherriff and And-erson. Therein lies the perpetuation of the myth. Everyone 'knows' for instance that Wallis waded into the sea to fish for broken bomb casings with his feet, that Gibson's entire crew transferred with him from his old unit to 617 Squadron, that all the bomb aimers used the wooden V-shaped bomb sight, and that David Maltby's Lancaster dropped the bomb that actually broke the Möhne Dam. In fact, of course, none of these things is completely true and some are completely wrong.

The resemblance to the truth however was close enough to make it hard for some people to see their loved ones recreated on the screen. My parents, my brother George and I travelled back from Malta in November 1954, when my father was posted back to Britain, and my brother Andrew was born in our new house in Plymouth in February 1955. I have no recollection of my parents going to see the film when it opened, although it must have been shown in cinemas in the city in the autumn of that year.

For Ettrick and Aileen 1955 was also the year when they began planning their retirement from Hydneye. Retirement would also mean cutting off many of their other local activities, which were largely sporting. Ettrick stood down from the committee of Sussex County Cricket Club and the Hastings Festival with its annual match against the Police. Aileen cut some of her hockey links, but remained a selector for the South and England for a number of years after that. They had decided to leave Hydneye at the end of the spring term in 1956, so the police cricket match in July 1955 was their last at the school. I recall a number of trips up and down from Plymouth to Hastings, which must have taken place about this time. My other grandparents, Lionel and Judith Foster, also lived in Hastings, and we would be taken to visit both families.

Every year, Christmas was the big event and, in his diary, Ettrick recorded who was present. There could be as many as 17 people for lunch, which would usually happen in the school dining room. That last Christmas, in 1955, my mother Jean must have been pregnant again, as my twin sisters were born in July 1956, but all Ettrick recorded was that she was ill in bed with thrombophlebitis.

Ettrick and Aileen were planning to move to Little Houghton in Northamptonshire, to a pair of cottages owned by Aileen's sister Mildred, which were being converted into one dwelling. In March Aileen paid a visit but work had hardly started. So after one more visit from the family at Easter, they stayed at Mildred's until the end of July, when the work was finished.

For the families of the other men lost in David's aircraft life also went on. They had not had the 'consolation', as Mrs Elizabeth Nicholson put it, of being able to bury their sons. All seven of them are now commemorated at the Air Forces Memorial in Runnymede, listed among the 20,456 men and women with no known grave, lost in operations flying from British soil. Michael Stone, who like me is a nephew of one of those killed that day, remembers being taken as a small boy to the dedication of the memorial by the Queen in October 1953, shortly after her coronation. His grandparents, Joseph and Dorothy Stone, did their best to keep Antony's memory alive, with Joe keeping the photo of him in RAF uniform on prominent display in his hairdresser's shop until he retired. His regular customers would have known the story well, but did he ever tire of explaining the picture and telling the story behind it to the casual caller? I would say not.

The Stones also gave a silver cup to the Winchester Air Cadets, to be awarded as a trophy each year to the outstanding cadet, but as local historian Alan Kinge found when he enquired after it in the early 1990s, none of the cadets or their officers knew anything about Antony, or why there was a cup named after him.

A certain amount of revisionism about the Dams Raid has occurred over the last two decades, with some authors and television researchers questioning whether it was a success or not. Many of these take their cue from a Channel 4 TV documentary in the early summer of 1993 made to coincide with the raid's 50th anniversary. In the later editions of his book, John Sweetman pithily demolishes most of the programme's criticisms, which were riddled with errors and sloppy research. (I remember watching the programme at the time and concerned at its negative approach, wrote down the day of transmission on a slip of paper. But preoccupied as I was with other matters, principally having become a father for the first time, in my 40s, three weeks earlier, I did nothing else.)

The programme concentrated on 617 Squadron's failure to destroy the Sorpe Dam, saying that it is much larger than the Möhne and Eder (which it isn't) and that unspecified 'men at the top' weren't listening when they were warned that Upkeep could not be used against it. In fact it was never planned to bounce Upkeep across the water towards the Sorpe. The two aircraft that did eventually attack it executed the manoeuvre given to them accurately, dropping the unspun mines while flying along the dam wall, allowing them to roll down and explode at depth. The fact that only two of the five scheduled to attack the Sorpe reached it can be put down to a combination of bad luck and accurate anti-aircraft fire by the German defences.

Critical programmes like these are often subsumed in general criticisms of British bombing tactics in the Second World War. However, as it was a precision raid on a key industrial target, the attack on the dams was not part of the area bombing strategy inherited and developed by Harris ('to bring the masonry crashing down on top of the Boche, to kill Boche and to terrify Boche'[101]) which has rightly been the subject of

---

101 Henry Probert, Bomber Harris, 2001, p.223, quoted in A C Grayling, Among the Dead Cities, Bloomsbury, 2007, p.119

much controversy. If we accept that bombing from the air is an acceptable tactic in war then surely an attack of this kind (which was not at all typical of Bomber Command's normal operations in May 1943) is perfectly justifiable. It has even been argued that the promotion of the success of the Dams Raid after the war could have helped alleviate the uncomfortable feeling that area bombing was a campaign of which the Allies should not be especially proud.[102]

It should be said that even though the Dams Raid was not an exercise in area bombing most of 617 Squadron would already have been engaged in this tactic on other raids. Many would not perhaps have expressed themselves as vehemently as their ultimate commander, Air Marshal Harris, but most of them would certainly have held the view that it was legitimate to bomb civilian targets, if for no other reason than revenge for the Blitz attacks on British cities. Guy Gibson expressed these thoughts trenchantly enough, arguing that it was revenge for German actions for more than a century and a half:

For year after year [the Germans] had waged war on defenceless European countries, bleeding them, starving them, murdering them. They had done this for one hundred and fifty years, and the German had never known what it was to have his own home destroyed. Wars had always been glorious, far from the fat Fräulein's doorstep.[103]

Gibson's cavalier approach to history (weren't the Prussians on the British side at Waterloo, a mere 130 years before the Second World War?) doesn't mean that his views were not widely shared. Even if it wasn't actually chalked on every bomb case by belligerent armourers, 'Take That Fritz' was the message delivered nightly by the Lancasters and Halifaxes of Bomber Command.

✳ ✳ ✳

Hydneye is gone now, with it the swimming pool, the cricket pitch and the memorial plaque which Ettrick and Aileen had placed inside it. The two cedar trees are apparently still there. My mother Jean died in 1987 and her sister Audrey in 2001. Nina, David's widow, remarried after the war and had two more children. She died in 2002. John, David and Nina's son, of course has no memory of a father who died when John

102 John Ramsden, *The Times*, 14 December 2002
103 Gibson, *Enemy Coast Ahead*, p.222

was just ten weeks old.

But the Dams Raid lives on, and now occupies a singular place in our history. It is an event about which everyone (at least above a certain age) knows something. A few people think they know a little more, and are often wrong. There is a small band of real experts, many of whom I have been fortunate enough to meet or correspond with in the course of writing this book, and who have been unfailingly generous with their time. There are other people who get in on the act. These range from downright dangerous nutters, like BNP supporters outside football grounds who follow lusty renditions of the Dambusters theme with racist chants about Pakis and Sieg Heil salutes, to art directors, copywriters, journalists and comedians. But are jokes about an event which cost the lives of 53 Allied aircrew and 1,341 German and other civilians appropriate? Do they exist about other similar events in either war?

It's possible to have some sympathy with the German newspapers in 1955 who regretted the making of a film that would merely add to 'the glorification of a gruesome act' of war. This is commented on by John Ramsden:

> The dams raid is certainly not remembered as a gruesome act by the British, rather as a consummate act of skill, bravery and sacrifice in a good cause – but these are not after all incompatible reactions to the same military event. In shaping that popular memory, The Dam Busters film was clearly, for good or ill, a key influence. But when all the analysis is over, it remains necessary to restate the central fact about that film: it remains, 50 years after being made, a film that is treasured because it is still so watchable, enjoyable and (for British and Commonwealth audiences, anyway) involving, moving and exhilarating.[104]

I am sure that, for the rest of their lives, Ettrick, Aileen and their immediate families recalled some aspects of the raid in a similar way. They would have seen it as a consummate act of skill and bravery, but I think they would not have gone along with the idea of sacrifice.

However, they – like the families of the other men who feature in this book – were not exceptional in losing a son, a brother, a husband, father or uncle in war. When I was a child I sometimes thought that

102 Ramsden, *Dam Busters*, p.123

having a relative involved in such a famous piece of history made our family somehow special, but now I realise that it is not so. We are no different from any other who lost someone in the war, male or female, military or civilian. Nearly every family in the country was touched in this way.

In Britain today, very fortunately, we do not have the experience of seeing large numbers of young people suddenly dying in their 20s. When a death does occur it happens to individual families or communities and is no less shocking for that. But there is an older generation: people who lived through a world war, like my mother, then a girl in her teens, and my grandparents, then in their 50s, the decade I am in now. We think of them as the 'make do and mend' generations, the people who hoarded old Christmas decorations in National Milk biscuit tins, and whose cheery Cockney banter helped them through the blitz. That may have been the spirit that helped them, but they must also have had the sickening, almost unbearable collective sense that a swath of young people had gone. That, more than the connection to an iconic piece of British history, was the experience that irrevocably shaped their lives, and their experience in its turn shaped mine.

Heroes

I remember talking to a friend who in the course of his work once had to ring John Arlott. 'Wow,' I said, knowing how much we had both revered him, 'what was that like?' He paused, and said slowly, thoughtfully: 'It was like speaking to God.' I never got to speak to the great cricket commentator, but several times I did have to ring another hero of mine, the historian Edward Thompson, about an introduction to a book I was producing. I was similarly tongue tied talking to someone whose work I had always admired, and whose political writing was so fluent and so sharp that it seemed wholly unjust that he wasn't more widely honoured.

It wasn't until a few years later that I read more about Thompson's own life, and discovered the story of how his older brother, a gifted writer, linguist, political activist and soldier, had died on a secret mission in Bulgaria in 1944. Several times in his own busy life, Edward Thompson tried to uncover the facts behind the death of his brother, who has been unjustly maligned as trying to foment some sort of political revolution as a romantic idealist and a latterday 'Lawrence of Bulgaria'. Sadly, Edward's own death prevented him finishing this research but his widow, Dorothy Thompson, also a historian of great renown, was able to put it together, based on a series of lectures he had given in the 1980s and his other work. It was published in 1997 as *Beyond the Frontier*. It's a short book, but a wonderful tribute to a lost brother and by extension a tribute to the determination to resist fascism so prevalent amongst his generation.

At the beginning of this book I quoted from a novel by Iris Murdoch, who had been in love with Frank Thompson while they were both at Oxford before the war. Murdoch, like the Thompsons, came from the same generation as David Maltby and my parents. Some of them survived the war, but they all were affected by the loss of those who did not. That they carried this burden for the rest of their lives is not in doubt.

Among Frank Thompson's papers was found a poem, Polliciti Meliora, which has since been much quoted and anthologised. I print it again here because it sums up the spirit of this remarkable generation who fought against tyranny, even if it took them to the point of self-sacrifice:

As one who, gazing at a vista
    Of beauty, sees the clouds close in,
And turns his back in sorrow, hearing
    The thunderclouds begin.
So we, whose life was all before us,
    Our hearts with sunlight filled,
Left in the hills our books and flowers,
    Descended, and were killed.
Write on the stones no words of sadness –
    Only the gladness due,
That we, who asked the most of living,
    Knew how to give it too.

I began this book with a quotation from Iris Murdoch. It seems appropriate to end it with another, from a poem called *The Agamemnon Class, 1939.*

The hero's tomb is a disputed mound.
What really happened on the windy plain?
The young are bored by stories of the war.
And you, the other young who stayed there
In the land of the past are courteous and pale,
Aloof, holding your fates.

For young people not to be 'bored by stories of the war' it is important that they know what their grandparents' generation did, why they fought, how they died. I have tried to tell the stories of just seven of these men, who by chance came to prominence as they took part in the most famous single operation ever undertaken by the Royal Air Force. But they were only seven out of the 120,000 who fought in Bomber

Command, and the millions, civilian as well as military, heroes all, who took part in the war itself. Those who died are forever in the shadows, 'courteous and pale'. Thanks to them, we are still in the sunlight, with lives to live.

A.J. McNALLY (CANADA)
D.J.H. MALTBY D.S.O. D.F.C.
J. MARRIOTT D.F.M.

J. FORT D.F.C.
C.L. FOX

W. HATTON
F.C. HAWKINS

K.A.J. HEWITT
V. HILL
S. HITCHEN

E.W. NICHOLS
V. NICHOLSON D.F.M.
J.P. NUGENT

A.J. STONE
C.S. STOUT D.F.C.

H.T. SIMMONDS
J.S. SIMPSON

Details from the 617 Squadron memorial, Woodhall Spa. PHOTO: CHARLES FOSTER

Acknowledgements

I t's been a strange experience writing this book. While some writers confess that they have used their books about the RAF and the war to rehearse their boyhood fantasies of battling with Jerry from the cockpit of a Spitfire or struggling through heavy flak to bomb the hell out of Berlin, my war games as a child were different. Heavily influenced by storylines like that of the film The Guns of Navarone I would fantasise about being some sort of commando dropped behind enemy lines – meeting partisans in remote mountain passes, lying in the undergrowth waiting to ambush troop convoys and so on.

I wasn't the flying nut in my family. I left that to my brother George, who finally realised his boyhood dreams by qualifying as a pilot at the age of 50. I've never had the desire to learn to fly, in much the same way as I've never wanted to learn to ski or strip a carburettor or play bridge. Writing this book has brought me into contact with the sorts of people who can tell the differences between B I and B III Lancasters. Many have been invaluable sources of information, but I feel a bit of a fraud in their company as I don't share the depth of their interests.

So in thanking people who have helped with this book, I'll start with my family. My brothers George and Andrew and my sisters Jane and Sarah have shared their family memories with me and corrected me on details. It was Andrew who unwittingly started me off on this book by alerting me to an interview with George Baker on the BBC's Today programme in December 2005, in which he told the story about David shooting the plates. I had never heard this before, and it spurred me into action. For a long time I had felt that if a member of my family was public property in this way, someone should document his life. It was at that moment that I realised how little I really knew about David's life, and indeed also about my mother's.

Other members of the extended Maltby, Hatfeild, Goodson and Foster families have also been of great assistance. My cousins Anthea Johnston and David Blackburn have encouraged the project the whole way through. As the oldest Maltby grandchild, Anthea deserves special thanks for preserving our grandfather's diaries and seeking out contact numbers and photographs. David Maltby's grandson, Charles Maltby has also been very helpful, as has Ralph Maltby's daughter, Rosamond Hills. Four of David's surviving first cousins, Mary Tapp, Frances Bonsey and Rachel Palmer (all Hatfeilds), and Ruth Walton (a Maltby) have generously shared their memories of the family. Jane Fanshawe helped with photos from the Walton collection. Charles Maltby (another Charles Maltby!) in South Africa, shared his memories of his uncle, Louis Maltby. The Goodson and Walter families, in the persons of Sue Snowden, Richard Walter and Michael Walter were very helpful. My godmother Mary Taylor-Jones kindly sent me original press cuttings and her copy of the *Tatler* magazine with the Cuthbert Orde drawings. My brother-in-law, niece and nephew Peter, Louise and Edward Phillips helped with research at the Imperial War Museum and National Archives. Simon Wainwright sent me press material he acquired in Lincolnshire all the way from Australia.

I would also like to thank the many archivists, librarians and museum curators who have helped with the research, including: Deborah Bircham (Grantham Museum), Jenny Christian (2nd Air Division Memorial Library, Norwich), Karen Parker and Prue Hatton (Winchester Museum), Sandy Mounsey (Winchester Local Studies Library), Mervyn Hallam (RAF Scampton Museum), Tony Meech (Margate Museum), Peter ver de Mato (Spitfire Memorial Museum, Manston), Katie Hanks (Wakefield Library).

Many other people have helped in various ways, and I am grateful to them: George Baker, Alan Kinge, John Sweetman, Alan Thompson, David Perkins (St Edward's School), Mrs Brenda House, Dave Bradley, Guy Voice, Paul Tritton, John Addley and Jack Wingate (East Kent Aircrew Association), Tony Overill, Richard Morris, Tobin Jones, Martin Johnson, Nick Stein, Stuart Roberts, Martin Waters.

Thanks are also due to members of the families of David's crews for answering many questions and supplying photographs and other material. In 617 Squadron: Valerie Ashton (née Hill), Grace Blackburn (née Simmonds), Cyril and Olga Nicholson, and Michael Stone. In 97 Squadron: Kevin Lancey.

I would like to salute the surviving members of 617 Squadron. They must all have been asked the same questions hundreds of times, and yet they continue to treat every enquiry with patience and courtesy.

Those kind enough to correspond with me were George Johnson, Grant Macdonald, Les Munro, Fred Sutherland, Fay Gillon and the late Harry Humphries. (Sadly Harry Humphries died shortly before this book went to press.) Thanks also to Harry Humphries and the Erskine Press for permission to reproduce material from Harry Humphries' book, *Living with Heroes;* to Dorothy Thompson for permission to reproduce Frank Thompson's poem, *Polliciti Meliora;* to the Iris Murdoch estate for permission to reproduce her poem, *The Agamemnon Class, 1939.*

Other RAF personnel, from outside 617 Squadron, who served with David during the war have also been generous with their time and assistance. These were Hugh Aitken, John (Tommy) Thompson and Bruce Ballantyne.

Thanks are also due to various historians and writers associated with Bomber Command and its squadrons. The author of the *Lancaster at War* books, Brian Goulding. Len Cairns, who kindly placed his research into the bombing of the Dortmund Ems canal at my disposal, and directed me to the relevant papers in the National Archives. From 617 Squadron, Alex Bateman, Jim Shortland and Paul Morley. From 9 Squadron, Roger Audis. From 97 Squadron, I owe a big debt to Kevin Bending, who has written a fine account of this squadron's war, *Achieve Your Aim,* which deserves much wider acclaim. Then there is Robert Owen, 617 Squadron's official historian, for whom the highest praise is not nearly enough. He has supplied much material, answered many obscure questions and checked many drafts, with the utmost diligence and courtesy.

Finally, my own immediate family: Jacqui, my wife, who has always been willing to critique my efforts and provide moral support. And my children, Patrick and Aisling, whose forbearance and sometimes not too gentle nagging was always a spur to finish the job. I hope they understand why I had to write this book.

Bibliography

A formal bibliography of the works consulted in the preparation and writing of this book follows, but I should begin by acknowledging five particular works which have been an enormous help, and on which I have relied most heavily. These are:

John Sweetman, *The Dambusters Raid,* Cassell Military, 2002. This is the authoritative account of the Dams Raid, and will surely never be surpassed as a work of record. Much of my account of the build-up, the raid itself and its aftermath derives from this book.

Richard Morris, *Guy Gibson,* Penguin, 1995. The most thorough biography of Gibson, which provides much of the background on how the Dambusters myth was first promulgated.

John Ramsden, *The Dam Busters,* Tauris, 2003. Ostensibly a book about the making of the film, in fact in just over 120 pages it covers the whole Dambusters story and much of the social history of the time.

Kevin Bending, *Achieve Your Aim,* Woodfield Publishing, 2005. Excellent history of 97 Squadron, from which I have unashamedly quarried most of the account of David's first tour of operations.

Harry Humphries, *Living with Heroes,* Erskine Press, 2003. Very helpful memoirs by the founder adjutant of 617 Squadron.

Other books consulted
Bishop, Patrick, *Bomber Boys,* Harper Press, 2007
Brickhill, Paul, *The Dam Busters,* Evans Brothers 1951
Calder, Angus, *The People's War,* Panther, 1972
Chorley, W R, *RAF Bomber Command Losses, Volume 4, 1943,* Midland, 1996
Connelly, Mark, *Reaching for the Stars,* Tauris, 2001
Cooper, Alan, *The Men who Breached the Dams,* Airlife, 2002
Euler, Helmuth, *The Dams Raid through the Lens,* After the Battle, 2001
Falconer, Jonathan, *The Dam Busters,* Sutton, 2003

Falconer, Jonathan, *Filming the Dam Busters,* Sutton, 2005

Faulks, Sebastian, *The Fatal Englishman,* Vintage, 1997

Garbett, Mike and Goulding, Brian, *Lancaster at War,* Ian Allan, 1971

Garbett, Mike and Goulding, Brian, *Lancaster at War 2,* Ian Allan, 1979

Gibson, Guy, *Enemy Coast Ahead,* Michael Joseph, 1946

Grayling, A C, *Among the Dead Cities,* Bloomsbury, 2007

Harrison, Stanley, *A Bomber Command Survivor,* Sage Pages, 1992

Hastings, Max, *Bomber Command,* Pan, 1999

Holt, Tonie and Valmai, *My Boy Jack,* Leo Cooper, 1998

Kirby, Robert, *The Avro Manchester: the legend behind the Lancaster,* Midland Publishing, 1995

Middlebrook, Martin and Everitt, Chris, *The Bomber Command War Diaries,* Midland Publishing, 1996

Overill, Tony, *Crash Boats of Gorleston,* Woodfield Publishing, 2005

Robertson, Bruce, *Lancaster: The Story of a Famous Bomber,* Harleyford, 1964

Sweetman, John, *Bomber Crew,* Abacus, 2005

Sweetman, John, Coward, David and Johnstone, Gary, *The Dambusters,* Time Warner, 2003

Taylor, James and Davidson, Martin, *Bomber Crew,* Hodder & Stoughton, 2005

Terraine, John, *The Right of the Line,* Hodder & Stoughton, 1985

Thompson, E P, *Beyond the Frontier,* Merlin, 1997

Tritton, Paul, *A Canterbury Tale: Memories of a classic wartime movie,* Tritton, 2000.

Ward, Chris, Lee, Andy and Wachtel, Andreas, *Dambusters,* Red Kite, 2003

Other works from which I have quoted are cited in the text.

In addition, I have consulted various records held by the National Archives, the RAF Museum and the Imperial War Museum. These are also cited where appropriate in the text.

Abbreviations used for Ranks

Various abbreviations have been used for RAF ranks over the years. In this book I have retained the orginal abbreviation where I am quoting from original sources. Otherwise I have used the following system:

Officers

Marshal of the Royal Air Force	
Air Chief Marshal	
Air Marshal	
Air Vice Marshal	
Air Commodore	Air Cdre
Group Captain	Gp Capt
Wing Commander	Wg Cdr
Squadron Leader	Sqn Ldr
Flight Lieutenant	Flt Lt
Flying Officer	Flg Off
Pilot Officer	Plt Off

Other ranks

Warrant Officer	WO
Flight Sergeant	Flt Sgt
Sergeant	Sgt
Leading Aircraftman	LAC
Aircraftman	AC
Aircraftman (2nd class)	AC2

Index